A Budding Success

The Ultimate Guide to Planning, Launching and Managing a Lucrative Legal Marijuana Business

By

C. Restivo & C. Cervantes

ISBN-13: 978-0-9978397-0-8

Table of Contents

Welcome!

Thanks for joining us in the brave new world of **legalized** medical marijuana distribution and consumption. We know you'll enjoy the experience.

It's a great time to consider starting a medical marijuana business because more and more states are moving towards legalization (for medical and recreational purposes). You can be on the cutting edge of entrepreneurship in a sector of the business world that is poised to explode at an exponential rate. The coming Green Revolution (or Cannabis Rush) is set to open the nascent marijuana industry up to EVERYONE— hundreds of millions of people across the United States will suddenly be allowed to partake (either for medical or recreational purposes) in something that has been illegal for a very long time. Imagine what that could mean for an established marijuana business when "the wall" does come down. Now it's legal to ship marijuana over state lines, so you can immediately incorporate mail order into your business model while everyone else is still in the early stages of setting up the business. You're already there and ready to take advantage of the sudden demand for legal marijuana. We applaud your interest in this industry and feel many opportunities exist.

There are other outcomes to imagine as well. Think about the rise of large-scale farming in the past twenty-five years. How did that occur? Simple. Large corporations bought up small farms (and we're talking about family farms here) and pooled their harvests to make millions, if not billions. Now think about that same model repeating itself twenty-five years down the road (if not sooner), only this time it's not corn, wheat, and soybeans. This time it's marijuana. You could own one of those businesses that are bought up by large corporations and realize huge profits from your efforts. Some people don't like the sound of that option.

If your motivations are less about money and more about working with a product you love, the medical marijuana industry is still for you. You might produce a strain organically, better than anyone else and not intend to ever sell out. You can make a great living with a unique product (or market) as well. It truly is the best of both worlds. That's the beauty of the American dream; you have the option to choose love, money, or both.

Whether used for medical purposes or recreation, pharmaceuticals are a big part of life in this country, and you can be involved in helping people get what they need and want more safely. Think about the love and loyalty for Apple/Mac products that are purchased by millions of users around the world. Don't you wish you could have been part of starting that business and building such love and loyalty, if for no other reason than you are working with a product of which you are a fan? (Forget the huge amounts of money you could have made had you invested in Apple when it first started.) You can get in on the ground floor with the sale of marijuana and be a part of the "next big thing" that will sweep the nation (and perhaps the world) in the next quarter-century. What a fabulous opportunity you have before you!

It's important to note that I will be addressing operations that could apply to both medical and recreational marijuana in states where distribution and consumption are legal. Be sure to check your local and state laws before embarking on any endeavor involving marijuana.

We refer to the product mainly as 'medical marijuana' because that is where most states start, with the legalization of marijuana for medical purposes. Medical marijuana takes on a variety of forms and often precedes recreational consumption. Recreational usage of marijuana is legal in a handful of states where adults of a certain age can freely buy and consume (similar to alcohol and tobacco). Most of our ideas can be applied to both medical marijuana and recreational marijuana businesses; we will identify items that strictly apply only to one or the other. Again, be sure to understand your local and state regulations before you determine the business venture you want to pursue.

Regardless of whether you want to work with medical marijuana, venture into the sale of recreational marijuana, or just work with an associated company, we are positive that starting and running your own business will be a rewarding experience. It might not be the easiest at times, but with due diligence and hard work, you are bound to succeed. There's nothing better than working with a product you whole-heartedly endorse while making money at the same time. Often, if you are working with passion and your primary goal is helping others, then the money will follow naturally.

We've enjoyed our marijuana ventures and have consulted with a number of businesses in various states. This book is intended to provide you with a foundation of knowledge for your marijuana venture. This should be a starting point of your search for information, not an ending point. Take the time to learn as much as you can (especially about the legal issues in your area) before starting your business so you can avoid future legal problems. Getting educated and playing it safe is never a bad thing.

Alright, let's get started.

Authors

Charles Restivo is an entrepreneur with a background in finance and accounting, including employment at high-end accounting firms in California. Early in his career, he spent a number of years auditing 501(c)(3) non-profit corporations and became familiar with internal operations. In his position at West End Partners, a local boutique investment firm that evaluated and partnered with failing businesses in order to restructure them, Mr. Restivo gained extensive knowledge of business valuation, acquisitions, and consulting. He is a UCSB graduate with an Honors degree in Economics.

Mr. Restivo has been a long-time medical marijuana advocate and has worked with a number of collectives over the last decade. His collective was awarded Santa Barbara's first official medical marijuana dispensary permit. Through this process, he gained a wealth of knowledge in the ever-evolving and still a somewhat controversial topic of medical marijuana dispensaries. He was a frontrunner establishing and running a successful storefront dispensary. He has gone on to help numerous others open dispensaries and/or streamline the processes.

Through his own experience in establishing and running a collective, Mr. Restivo has had interactions with local police, district attorneys, and federal DEA officers. Fortunately, these confrontations ended in only one minor possession violation. However, these interactions were an integral part of his learning process. Mr. Restivo has heard first-hand what the other side, the prosecuting district attorneys, consider "legal" and what specific details they are currently focusing on to pursue legal action. His numerous hours in court sessions and attorney briefings provide him with a unique, even priceless, perspective on the medical marijuana laws.

1

Mr. Restivo has devoted himself to attendance at medical marijuana conferences and relevant government meetings and has extensively researched marijuana politics over the last decade. He wrote his first successful CA medical marijuana guidebook in 2012, which received high praise and is currently featured in two prominent law libraries.

Currently, Mr. Restivo continues to consult with individuals opening dispensaries, Medical Marijuana (MMJ) delivery services, as well as other private businesses, retail boutiques, and entertainment companies.

Cory Cervantes grew up near Seattle, Washington, and moved to Southern California in the late 1990s, where he became intrigued with the sprouting medical marijuana scene. His cannabis career started in the early 2000s, when he operated a hydroponics store and quickly immersed himself in the MMJ industry. Mr. Cervantes assumed a variety of responsibilities over the next decade, including day-to-day dispensary operations, employee training, patient interaction and retention, city compliance, local licensing, oversight of large outdoor grows, extraction, and edibles manufacturing.

Building on his success as a grower, Mr. Cervantes became a consultant to multiple cannabis farms in California. He has managed multiple indoor and outdoor grow operations on the West Coast. He was instrumental in the construction and operations of two cannabis dispensaries in Santa Barbara. Mr. Cervantes has also refined operating procedures for an edibles company and helped with its branding.

As the MMJ scene evolved, Mr. Cervantes started a private consulting group. Through this entity, he has worked with a number of clients to develop business plans, dispensary outlines and staffing, workflow structures, employee handbooks, product selection processes, and growing procedures. He has also supported various MMJ applications and worked with businesses to secure retail dispensary or wholesale licenses in California, Nevada, and Washington.

Mr. Cervantes recently designed the dispensary layout and operating procedure for the Suquamish Tribe in WA. Currently, he manages one of the longest-standing cannabis collectives and delivery services in the California Tri-Counties area.

The information contained in this guide is for informational purposes only. Any legal or financial advice that we provide is our opinion (only) based on our personal experiences. You should always seek the advice of a legal professional before acting on something that we published or recommended. Users of this guide are advised to do their own due diligence when it comes to making business decisions and all information, products and services that have been provided should be independently verified by your own qualified professionals. By reading this guide, you agree that we are not responsible for the success, failure, and possible criminal violations of your (or your organization's) decisions as they relate to any information presented in this guide. You shall assume all responsibility for any actions associated with our advice.

Introduction

The goal of this manual is to provide readers with the tools they need to get started in the medical marijuana industry. If you have started a business in the past, you may find some of this information redundant; however, we didn't want to leave any information uncovered. This book offers the most current information available, but check the web (we suggest NORML.org as a starting point) for up-to-the-minute changes.

In this book, we delve deeply into dispensary operations, from current laws to day-to-day operations, as well as how to comply with the various state agencies. Our approach is to provide you with as many resources as we can in order for you to successfully open and operate a medical marijuana dispensary (or grow operation) under the guidelines set forth by your state.

We strongly suggest that you read the book from beginning to end before you make any business decisions and that you take notes and flag areas to re-read as questions arise. However, if you need a quick answer, refer to the table of contents for a specific topic. As you may know, the medical marijuana industry is constantly evolving and your search for knowledge should not stop with this or any other book. Thank you for purchasing this book, and we hope you are pleased with the information we have provided. We also encourage you to submit feedback.

As a starting point, if you are looking to get into medical marijuana (and its usage), this needs to be treated much differently than recreational marijuana (which is still *illegal* in most states). There are very specific guidelines that need to be followed to ensure that any marijuana activities you take part in are classified as being for medical purposes only. Please note that although dispensaries require business-like qualities to survive, some states require **not-for-profit** entities that are very complex while at the same time fundamental for operating in this industry.

Since medical marijuana has become legal, thousands of people have gotten involved in the new industry for a number of reasons. Some are marijuana activists who strongly believe in the medicinal use of the product. Others are people who use medical marijuana and want better, safer access to it. Still others simply enjoy the uplifting effects of marijuana. Many people are attracted to the business side—the opportunity to be self-employed, the flexible hours, and the excitement of being at the forefront of an emerging industry that has billion-dollar yearly potential. **Please note that while some are attracted to the potential for financial gain, your written plans must comply with the state in which you reside. Some states require a not-for-profit objective.** This doesn't mean that you can't make a decent living from this industry, but you need to be cognizant of your earnings and make sure you are in compliance. This may require some due diligence and documentation to back up your earnings. Work to create a cash flow positive business and hope that your main issue is excess cash!

With that being said, here is a summary of what you will need to do to get started in the medical marijuana industry:

1. Review and fully understand your state's guidelines.
2. Decide what medical marijuana profession you wish to become involved in:
   a. Cultivate medical marijuana and sell it to patients or dispensaries.
   b. Process cannabis into medical marijuana, concentrates, edibles, and topicals.
   c. Deliver medical marijuana to patients. NOTE: Be sure to check your state's status.
   d. Operate a storefront dispensary that functions like a pharmacy for medical marijuana.

    e. Consider adding non-MMJ products or services (more on IRS 280E later).

3. Get organized:
    a. Brainstorm—create goals for your collective or your cultivation.
    b. Research current local, county, and state MMJ laws.
    c. Pull together an operating team of qualified individuals (if applicable).

4. Choose an entity for your business (or not-for-profit, if applicable).

5. Create a collective or cooperative corporation (if applicable).
    a. Keep detailed records of:
       i. Entity formation.
       ii. Corporate formalities (bylaws, agreements, minutes of meetings).
       iii. Keep an accurate accounting of income and expenses.
       iv. Keep copies (or digital records) of receipts.

6. Get a doctor's recommendation to use and grow medical marijuana (if applicable in a medical marijuana state).
    a. Track time donated by members.
    b. Ensure that all transactions fall within the state law.

Overview

The ever-evolving medical marijuana industry started in California and has been around since 1996. Since then, more states have legalized medical marijuana (and recreational marijuana), creating new opportunities for entrepreneurial growth. Throughout this time, the industry has endured in an unclear legal atmosphere, and the interpretation and enforcement of laws vary widely from state to state and county to county. **Regardless of where you (plan to) operate, it is mandatory that you stay aware of current laws at the state, county, and city levels.** Also, please be politically active and promote the positive aspects of marijuana whenever possible.

The medical marijuana industry has recently been described as the modern-day gold rush. Many people got excited about the industry and, given all the positive press (and economic data), we don't blame them. In 2011, CNBC aired its *Marijuana, Inc.* documentary nationwide, which it updates and rebroadcasts repeatedly. The program showed people growing giant plants in Northern California with little fear of prosecution. In 2015, CNBC aired *Marijuana America: Colorado Pot Rush*, showing sophisticated grow operations and processing facilities in Colorado. Marijuana is quickly evolving from a shunned "drug" to an alternative medicine and socially accepted recreational drug much like alcohol or tobacco.

Take, for example, the state of Washington. Marijuana retailers there are enjoying huge profits from the legalization of the plant. The website www.502data.com (which reports state legal WA sales figures) reported the top two marijuana dispensaries are earning almost $1.5 million per month and growing! More than a dozen shops are earning $500,000 or more per month. And dozens more are earning more than $100,000 every month.

Here's another interesting statistic: one dispensary sold a total of $1,410,095 in all of 2014. In 2015, that same dispensary sold $15,765,779. That's a 1018% increase! And that's just one dispensary. The list literally goes on and on. Granted, excise tax can get a bit steep with these numbers (35%), but with a monthly sale of $1,336,604 (and an excise tax of $494,543), the dispensary still pulls in $842,061 for that month. Not bad for a retail establishment that only made $1.5 million total the year before.

Other states are no different. Colorado's state website (www.colorado.gov) reports that the total of all marijuana taxes, licenses, and fees in November of 2015 amounted to $12,231,410. That's a 64% increase over November of 2014 (which reported $7,465,568 in total taxes, licenses, and fees).

From these numbers (and websites) you can get an idea of the potential for a successful business, as well as the competition that could begin to grow between businesses that dispense marijuana. The numbers are showing that the marijuana industry is set to grow rapidly in the next few years (if it hasn't already started) as more states continue to address the issue of legalization. In actuality, "gold rush" may be a bit of a misnomer. Sure, there's going to be a rush to capitalize on the newly legal marijuana industry, but, unlike gold and other precious metals, marijuana isn't going to run out. It's a renewable resource. The coming Cannabis Rush has the potential to continue for a long time as more and more people see the benefits of marijuana use.

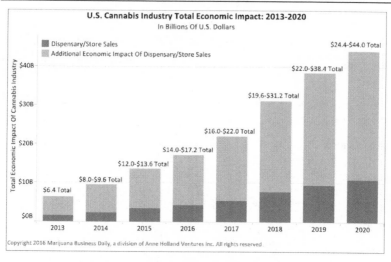

MMJ Business Factbook 2016

The debate regarding the full legalization of marijuana in the United States continues. Tensions at state and federal level are evident with neither party keen to force the issue. The publication MMJ Business Factbook 2016 raises the 'multiplier effect' in the broader economy per the above chart. Note the tremendous growth in the economy created from the dispensary sales. Imagine what would happen with Federal legalization.

As the economy continues to languish with no early end seemingly in sight, local politicians are going to continue to search for fresh impetus to stimulate their economies. Sales tax on medical marijuana in compliant states already justifies the administrative costs. When the multiplier effect on the tax base doubles this and new jobs appear in increasing numbers, we wonder how much longer the states will hold out. The statistical evidence is clearly there already.

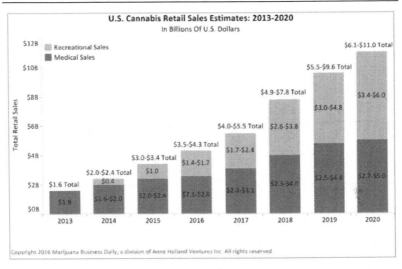

MMJ Business Factbook 2016

In 2016, we see a lot of consolidation, with a number of states poised to legalize medical marijuana and at least four states actively pursuing recreational usage. Experience suggests that the two years following will be periods of shaking down and consolidation. There will undoubtedly be a cap on the number of licenses per city (and not all cities will comply). Following that, sales will likely spike suddenly. You should consider ways to get ahead of the curve and secure a place in the sun.

You can get involved early and be ready to reap the same rewards that those mining, oil, or steel tycoons did in the 19th century. Start your marijuana retail establishment now before marijuana becomes the new coffee and there's a dispensary on every corner.

But before you rush out and start selling from your front porch or out of the back of a van, remember that even though the sale of marijuana may be legal (in some states), it is still heavily regulated and taxed (as you can see from the examples of Washington and Colorado above). What's more, chances are, every city and state are going to have different regulations, so it's important to be well-versed in the law; this is so you can operate a legal business and avoid the problems that come with run-ins with the law and the judicial system.

One of the most important things to watch for is strict regulatory compliance. Agencies continue to require strict attention to details from marijuana related ventures—typically with much more red tape than a traditional small business. You can win if you hold fast and stick to the rules. In Colorado in 2015, for example, 47% of infractions were for physical infrastructure and rules for specific licenses, with labeling and packaging errors increasingly under the spotlight.

When legalization takes place, a scarce license will become a hot commodity. Depending on your timing and location, you could be set up for massive growth. The medical marijuana industry already has over 1.5 million registered patients, and this can only increase (exponentially with recreational).

The first section of this book will highlight the importance of "being legal" and walk you through the basics of marijuana law. We cannot address all the local laws and regulations (the book would be just too big and impossible to stay current), so it's up to you to do your own research in order to comply with the laws where you intend to run your business. It may seem like a huge hurdle to contend with, but once established and legal, you'll be on your way to financial freedom working with a product you love. Let's get started!

Chapter 1: The Law

Laws are the foundation of our society and we must follow them to avoid various repercussions. State and federal legislation regarding medical and recreational marijuana will continue to be dynamic, so it's essential to stay on top of changes in your area. If you fail to do so, then you run the risk of losing your business and even your freedom.

Federal Law

The federal government viewed marijuana in all its forms as a schedule I narcotic (the same level as heroin and cocaine). Washington adopted the Controlled Substances Act in 1970, thereby making it unlawful to manufacture, distribute, dispense, or possess any controlled substance including marijuana. In August 2016, the DEA again denied re-scheduling cannabis based on recommendations from the U.S. Food and Drug Administration.

If cannabis becomes a schedule II drug, this will allow for research and clinical trials. This would have a huge impact on the overall industry and only time would tell of the full impact. A move to schedule III or lower would allow for marijuana suppliers (that are abiding by state laws) to deduct their business expenses, thereby solving one of the industry's major financial problems. Congressional action would be required to "legalize marijuana" or decriminalize cannabis completely but is pretty far off at this point, as U.N. international drug control treaties would need to be addressed as well. These treaties currently allow for regulated use of cannabis for medical purposes.

Some are pessimistic and are scared that this de-scheduling will bring in large pharmaceutical companies that would take over the industry. Some regulation experts say that when cannabis gets placed in the same category as other pharmaceutical drugs, the burden of keeping up with regulatory compliance might be too much for many of today's small marijuana businesses. There is no doubt that the impacts would be significant, but it will take years to evolve; plus, we don't feel the desire for small boutique cannabis businesses (and products) will ever go away.

State Law

Almost half of America's states already regulate medical marijuana, and more than a few are moving in the direction of allowing limited amounts of pot for recreational usage. This situation is still in a state of flux because these measures are dependent on what happens on Capitol Hill in Washington, D.C.

City & County Law

At the city level, the interest is in promoting an orderly urban structure through property rights, zoning, and ensuring health regulation compliance. Local ordinances have addressed the operations of dispensaries, cultivation, and/or delivery of medical marijuana. The attitude of local politicians will vary depending on their positions on marijuana use.

Priority of Compliance

It's essential to follow a top-down approach whereby you first meet the requirements in your applicable state and county before attending to the niceties of city planning. You don't want to build a dispensary to city guidelines only to find you can't sell there under county and state exemption laws.

Work through the county regulations before finding a spot where you can set up business.

In this regard, we urge you not to buy property, sign a lease, or make any legal agreements until you have met (or at least fully understand) the requirements at county and state level. It is much easier to fight a city violation (about signage, hours of operation, or other zoning issues) than it is to fight the state over more pertinent issues.

Chapter 2: Opportunities in the Cannabis Industry

6 Paths of Self-Employment with Cannabis

There are six general paths to being self-employed in the cannabis/MMJ industry. Most of these involve "touching the plant" or the delivery of product to the end user (or a combination thereof). However, the industry also provides a large number of opportunities for auxiliary businesses, and these will evolve with the industry as a whole. These are the main paths subject to the law in your particular state:

- Cultivate medical marijuana and sell it to patients or dispensaries.
- Process flowers into medical marijuana, concentrates, edibles, and topicals.
- Deliver medical marijuana to patients. {NOTE: Be sure to check your state's status on this.}
- Operate a storefront dispensary that functions like a retail drug store.
- Auxiliary business (from making a smoking/vaping device, cannabis testing facility, creating a cannabis tourism business, or marijuana related app).
- Passive investing in a medical marijuana business.

Your choice of one of the above or a combination will depend on the following issues.

Financing

How much cash do you need to start the business? (See Chapter 4 for budgeting.) Are you planning to self-fund, borrow money, or bring on investors (if applicable)? Luckily, this is a great time to seek private financing as investors see the growth and opportunity in this industry.

Ongoing Legal Compliance

These concerns apply to all paths, because continued operations depend on compliance with laws. How legal are you now? Who is in charge of watching for changes in legislation? What is your plan in case of an inspection/audit? Have you allocated responsibilities appropriately?

Where to Cultivate Medical Marijuana

Marijuana needs specific conditions to cultivate and also be out of the public eye. Where is the best place to cultivate it in your surrounding area? Are you considering indoor, outdoor, and hybrid cultivating methods? What prices can you expect from specific strains? If you're just starting out, should you try to buy or lease property? How much do you expect to payout before harvest? Does the landowner need to know you are cultivating?

Process Cannabis into Medical Marijuana, Concentrates, and Edibles

Where will you get the cannabis? How do you keep your product secure? What is the process for disposing of byproducts and waste? Do you have a system to protect product quality and maintain standards?

Deliver Medical Marijuana to Patients

Delivery services are easier to start than most of the other business ventures mentioned. How much product and how many strains should you start with? (Typically, quality is more important than variety.) Is there a maximum amount of product you should carry on each delivery? Who is in charge of money management? How do you keep cash secure? Who keeps books/records, and how do you stay compliant?

Operate a Storefront Dispensary

Dispensary success ultimately depends on sales. Where is your ideal location? Does it matter if your dispensary is not on a street with heavy traffic? How many patients/clients do you have, and how many can you serve? How many patients do you need before you pass breakeven point (where all expenses are paid for), and you start making a profit?

If you just want to get your feet wet, then there are also a number of opportunities to work at a dispensary; typical positions include clerical, accounting, green room tender, and on-site medical marijuana expert. Depending on the size of the collective, one person might be responsible for a number of duties.

Cultivating Medical Marijuana vs. Running a Dispensary

As discussed above, there are a number of ways to get involved in the medical marijuana industry. The two most common activities are to run a dispensary (retail) or cultivate medical marijuana (wholesale). These two activities are intertwined and require each other to survive. It is possible to do both of these activities, but keep in mind that your time is limited; you will likely have to determine what you are more interested in doing and which activity your skills are best suited for. In general, growing medical marijuana is much simpler (from a paperwork standpoint) than organizing and running a dispensary, which requires following a number of regulations while handling all the headaches of a typical medical office/retail store.

Growing requires spending a lot of time alone with the plants. Running a dispensary is a much more social endeavor and requires a lot of face time with patients. You will need to weigh the pros and cons to determine where you see the best fit for yourself. After reading this book, you should have a much better understanding of what is required for both of these activities.

Advantages of Cultivating	Advantages of Having a Dispensary
Simpler to Start-Up	Potential to Earn More Money
Solitary Working Environment	Social Working Environment
Greater Flexibility & Freedom	Chance to Create Jobs in Community
Less Start-up Capital Needed	Possibility of Sharing Costs
Grow Medicine for Yourself	Sell Product to Other Patients

Auxiliary business

Auxiliary (or support) businesses are often overlooked in this industry. However, there is a large opportunity in this segment. According to Marijuana Business Factbook 2016, these businesses have an average profit margin of 30%, which is higher than an average retail dispensary and equivalent to wholesale cultivators!

Auxiliary businesses are one step away from touching the plant and are a safer bet from a legal standpoint. This also makes it easier to scale/expand to multiple states and jurisdictions. Some of these companies/products can also serve other industries, adding to the underlying strength of this sector.

Some of the most common auxiliary businesses would include:

- Cultivation Support (grow lights, grow structures, grow medium, fertilizers—basically anything to do with the growth cycle or harvest of the plant).
- Cannabis testing facility.
- Software (any tools/apps/databases used to assist in either the growing or retail end of the business).
- Packaging.
- Consumption devices (pipes, rolling paper, vaporizers, etc.).
- Security and surveillance.
- General business services specifically aimed at MJ niche industry (legal, marketing, accounting, banking, education/training, web, etc.).

Investing in Medical Marijuana

Some investment gurus are comparing medical marijuana opportunities to the 1849 Gold Rush that lead to the declaration of the state of California. There were three types of beneficiaries in those days: the miners (who did the work), the bartenders and ladies (who entertained the miners), and the investors (who bankrolled the business).

As marijuana becomes more and more mainstream—and universal legalization more likely—the possibility of making relatively large sums of money through direct investment becomes better and better. If California is budgeting $134 million in tax revenue, then how much money do you think is changing hands in the marketplace? In general, a direct investment in a private company seems a better prospect, as public companies are more restricted in their activities.

Finding a Good Direct Investment

A special assessment is required before making an investment in the emerging medical marijuana industry. Some operators lack a business background; many are emerging entrepreneurs who have been growing medical marijuana in their backyards or with small collectives. They may lack the ability to promote their operations or skill set and often don't have clear plans how to grow the business efficiently.

There are a growing number of private equity funds that invest in private marijuana companies. Some of the current top companies include The ArcView Group, Privateer Holdings, Green Growth Investments, and Tress Capital. The problem with these types of firms is that they typically are only open to accredited investors (ones with a net worth of at least one million U.S. dollars, excluding the value of one's primary residence, or those who have an income of at least $200,000 each year for the last two years), leaving this option open to only a small percentage of the population.

Partnering or investing in Indian reservations/Native American tribes is another avenue with potential. In 2014, the U.S. Justice Department ruled that Native Americans can legally grow and sell marijuana on their sovereign lands. According to Cheryl Shuman, who works in private licensing, media, and real estate, 78,000 acres of Native American ground are now being used to grow marijuana. Also, special tax credits may be available for investors that make capital investments on Indian reservations.

Investing in Public Marijuana Stocks

Investing in public marijuana companies is gaining in popularity as more states begin to consider legalization. In 2015, this sector rose by double digits, giving credence to the legitimacy of the opportunity. However, this space has seen a lot of volatility. The Viridian Cannabis Stock Index (www.viridianca.com), composed of 50 to 75 publicly traded companies, saw a growth of 38.4% in 2014, followed by a loss of 32.4% in 2015.

Big names are getting involved in the action. PayPal co-founder Peter Thiel got involved in the growing industry by investing in several private marijuana start-ups through his San Francisco-based venture capital firm, Founders Fund.

That doesn't mean you have to be wealthy to get in the game. Penny stocks and micro-cap start-ups—many based in Canada where medicinal marijuana is legal—can provide significant rates of return when the dust settles, and marijuana is more widely accepted in the United States.

Please note that some over-the-counter (OTC) publicly traded companies have jumped on the bandwagon to try and make a quick buck from the marijuana boom. These are often smaller shell companies that recently changed their names and may have a sketchy financial history. They don't have any real business and are just trying to get a temporary pop from the momentum of this industry—so due diligence is required.

If investing in public companies that grow and sell marijuana has you a bit nervous, then other opportunities exist surrounding the industry's many ancillary businesses.

Investing in consulting (capitalizing on the need for licensing and business optimization), biotech, real estate, and software that is directly applicable to the marijuana industry can be a great way to expand your portfolio without the risk of investing in marijuana directly.

If you're interested in marijuana stock investment, public companies in these sectors are required to file 10-Q reports, which are in the public domain. These are a great source of financial information and quarter-to-quarter comparisons. A good place to start is Google or Yahoo Finance. Here you can get summary information and dig deeper into detailed company filings. These reports (and the information they contain) enable the shrewd investor to perform detailed research and identify real opportunity (vs. smoke and mirrors).

Chapter 3: Planning and Entity Selection

Do you need to create an entity, and if so, what type?

So you likely know the main business types: sole proprietor, partnership, LLC, and corporation. What is the best option? Unfortunately, there isn't an easy answer, and this will vary by your specific circumstance. A sole proprietor is the easiest to create, and it is basically starting a business personally where you hold all responsibility and all the liability. A partnership is almost the same thing but with more than one person (no liability protection), and a separate tax return is typically required. LLCs and corporations are popular in that they limit the liability to the entity and cannot (under most circumstances) hold the individuals responsible for debts.

LLCs are typically simpler to form and maintain than a corporation and have become the default choice for many new businesses. As mentioned, the LLC provides protection for its owners so that they do not become personally liable for any debts the LLC may incur. In addition, the LLC offers more choice where taxes are concerned. For example, an LLC owned by one person can choose to pay taxes as if he were a sole proprietorship but still take advantage of the liability protection of the LLC. This means that a one-person marijuana LLC operating out of the home can write off all expenses associated with a home office, utilities used by the business, and any sundries (cars, office supplies, etc.) used for business purposes.

A corporation is required to follow some specific rules on a periodic basis (at least annually) in order to retain its legal status. Not following these corporate formalities can jeopardize the recognition (or legitimacy) of the entity. You can't just set it up and forget it. A corporation requires ongoing maintenance to survive.

Corporations can take different forms and usually fall into one of two types: C corporation or S corporation. While most of the differences are legal or tax related, they all provide a level of protection that cannot be found with the sole proprietorship or the partnership (the two simplest forms of business entity). The main benefits of incorporating include tax advantages, limited liability, and easy ownership transfer. The tax advantages are perhaps the biggest incentive to incorporate. Under federal law, businesses can take advantage of deductions that aren't available to sole proprietors, partnerships, or LLCs and can potentially pay less taxes if done properly.

For example, when filing taxes, a corporation files a separate return. A shareholder employee (e.g., the owner) pays taxes only on his wages and half of his (or her) Social Security and Medicare taxes. The corporation pays the other half of those two taxes but can then deduct half of that half. If the owner is not an employee but merely a shareholder, then he only pays taxes on the dividends received that year (if any). The problem with a traditional C-corp is that the profits are taxed at the corporate level, and the dividends are also taxed at the shareholder level (aka double taxation). However, if the C-corp profits are less than $50K, then they are taxed at a low 15%. In the case of an S-corp, a shareholder who is also an employee can reduce self-employment tax by splitting profits between wages and shareholder distributions. S-corp distributions are only taxed at the shareholder level.

Though you might expect such legal entities to be difficult to create, the reality is quite different. Often it takes nothing more than a visit to your secretary of state's office or website, a bit of paperwork (i.e., articles of incorporation or organization), and a small fee (e.g., $50). You will also want to file for a federal employer identification number (EIN), but this can be done online or by printing out a form and mailing it in (once you have received your Articles from the state). You can do all of this yourself with materials available online or from Nolo.com. We go into more detail later in this chapter. For more handholding, websites like Legalzoom.com can handle these filings for a few hundred dollars. However, it may be worth your time and money to consult with a qualified attorney and/or CPA (especially if you are unsure which entity is required or will best suit your needs).

Collectives, Cooperatives, and Dispensaries Defined

The medical marijuana situation is likely to remain fluid for some time, with federal authorities and individual states taking up different positions regarding legality. Each state has its unique requirements for how a marijuana business can be organized. The terms 'collectives,' 'cooperatives,' and 'dispensaries' are not always consistently used.

- A **collective** is a group of patients that band together to provide their common MMJ needs. Some may grow, while others may process. Still others may finance the operation. In a closed circle, at least in theory, supplying members of the collective only, <u>at breakeven</u>.
- A **cooperative** is a <u>non-profit</u> organization or grouping of people that provides medical marijuana to its members and other patients in a retail-type environment. It can cultivate the flowers, process them, and sell them. All the proceeds go back into the organization or are distributed among the members.
- A **dispensary** is a physical location or storefront where medical marijuana is distributed. It is a retail sales location that can operate as either for profit or not for profit.

A collective or cooperative can operate a dispensary, but that is not always the case. Some states allow for profit entities (Individuals, LLCs, or Corporations) to open dispensaries. As the marijuana situation unfolds and states permit recreational use, the applicability of these definitions may blur further. It is thus essential to remain up to date with relevant rules and trends, so you are in a position to benefit quickly as regulations ease.

Planning and Organizing Your Entity

Step 1 – Goal Setting

The best way to achieve consensus within your organization is to agree on a written plan that outlines your ideas and goals. Depending on where you plan to operate and the laws prevailing there, you might also need to provide a business/operating plan to the city as part of their application process. You can create an outline for yourself and a more detailed version for the city or other outside parties as you deem appropriate. If you are opening a low-profile (smaller, non-advertising) delivery service, your outline will not require as much detail.

Step 2 - Brainstorming

Write down all your ideas without considering whether they are good or bad. Do not evaluate them at this stage—you will refine your list later. Generate ideas of what you want and how you are going to get there.

Try to build on these ideas by combining, merging, and separating issues into logical blocks, and then order them into a sequence. Remember to seek advice from members, directors, and any individuals inside the industry. There will likely be debates with different positions taken.

Step 3 - Creating a Mission Statement

This is a short written statement of the purpose of your entity. If you are stuck for ideas, find inspiration from charities on the Internet. The result should ideally contain all the elements of the following illustrative example:

To provide the highest quality of medicinal products and services to our members while supporting the legalization of marijuana.

Creating a Business Plan

A business plan is a formal statement of business goals and plans for reaching them. It may also contain background information about the state of the market and the organization or team attempting to achieve the objectives. This is probably one of the most important steps towards making money from medical or recreational marijuana.

The better your plan, the more likely you are to raise finances, sleep better at night, and run a successful operation. Don't think you can knock this off your to-do list on a Sunday afternoon. Business plans are not easy, and the average person will feel uncomfortable producing one. Though it requires a lot of thought and effort, in the end, a business plan makes things easier.

Executive Summary

This section tells the reader who you are, what the current circumstances of the organization are, and what you want it to become. It is a concise overview of the entire plan along with summary information about the directors/founders. (This will have some crossover with the vision statement.)

Main Document

1. Market Analysis

You need to do specific research on the market(s) in which you will operate. Who needs your services? Why are you targeting the sector(s)? What competitive organizations will you face? These questions need to be answered in the market analysis.

2. Organization and Management

Here you describe the organizational structure and outline how the organization will function. This could be an LLC, corporation, partnership, collective, or cooperative depending on your circumstances.

The management section should include background on the founders and what skills they bring to the endeavor. This section should also detail each position in the organization and associated responsibilities.

Allocate the talent you have to the leadership and management positions in the structure. If there are gaps in the structure, then develop a list of ideal qualities for vacant positions as the basis for your recruitment plan.

3. Operations

This section contains a broad description of how your organization is going to function. Discuss the nature of your organization and list the primary factors that you believe will make it a success. Identify the marketplace needs that you are trying to satisfy, and detail the ways in which you plan to achieve this.

4. Products and Services

The content of this section will depend on whether you are supplying medical or recreational marijuana, whether you are a collective or cooperative organization, and whether you will be selling related products and services (e.g., smoking devices, recipe books, etc.).

5. Marketing / Member Outreach

You are not going to become wealthy waiting for members or customers to find you. You will need to work to get your name out in the marketplace. That's where the marketing/member-outreach section comes into play. Typically, this section consists of public relations, personal promotion, social networks, and printed materials.

Once you define your membership goals, develop a marketing strategy to match. Periodically evaluate your efforts by questioning new patients and customers (this is the easy way), but be careful how you present your organization to the public.

In recent elections, opinion is still split down the middle when voting for or against legalization of marijuana for medicinal or recreational use. Your best marketing strategy is to produce professional-looking ads and focus on helping patients with their medical needs rather than getting people stoned silly (the recreational side).

Make sure any advertising clearly states that your organization is fully compliant with state laws and regulations. You will have less trouble if you advertise in marijuana-friendly media, but the more conservative outlets are becoming more accepting as time goes by.

6. Financial Plan / Start-Up Funding

Who is going to fund the start-up costs of your dispensary or collective? How much money do you need? A lender or investor is going to want to see an assurance that you have specific uses for the funding. Outline the required funds needed to:

    a. Get the collective running so the cash starts flowing in to buy more inventory.

    b. Cover your ongoing operating expenses until reaching a break-even point.

Please refer to the budget section for more advice on figuring out how much money you should seek. A business plan is more impressive when the owners/members are putting their own money in (as part of the initial investment). That said, you might need to seek top-up funding from outside investors. It is always a good idea to discuss specifics with a qualified attorney before accepting funding because some states prohibit investors from owning equity or profit sharing in a marijuana business.

If you form a cooperative corporation, then you have the ability to issue preferred shares to members who you pay a given rate of interest. The law limits the rate of return and payments must be regular. This can make using this funding option difficult if your cash flow slows.

You most likely won't have a lot of information to plug into all six items listed above on your first pass. Instead, start by focusing on your experience and background as well as the decisions that led you to start this particular entity. Include information about the problems your target market has and what solutions you can provide. Show how the expertise you have will allow you to make significant inroads into the market. Describe your goals and convince people to jump aboard with you.

Create a Vision Statement

Organizations can also benefit by creating a vision statement. A **vision statement** is a picture of your future endeavor (cultivation or dispensary), but more than that, your vision statement is your inspiration, the structure for all your planning. **The vision statement is typically more detailed and focused on future goals than the closely related mission**

statement. A vision statement may apply to you alone or to the entire collective. Whether for all or part of an organization, the vision statement answers the question: "Where do we want to go?"

Your vision statement is your dreams and hopes for the business. With it, you can regularly go back to your original vision and make sure you are staying on the right track. While a vision statement doesn't tell you how you're going to get there, it does set the basis for your operation planning.

When crafting a vision statement, you should use your imagination and dream big. Tap your passion for starting this business and map out your ideal situation. Refer to your mission statement and core competencies as a starting point for articulating your vision and values. The vision statement should also document where you see your project years from now. It should have an influence on decision-making starting on day one and help with your allocation of resources. Unfortunately, you need to keep in mind that there is the potential for law enforcement and the court system to read this statement, so be smart when you create it.

Remember, in creating your vision statement, be sure to address this question: How can your operation be better than all the others you have seen?

Get a Mentor

Ideally, you already know someone in the medical marijuana business who you can ask for advice. The more people you can bring together to help with the formation of your entity, the better it will be in the end. It is important, though, that everyone understands their role in the dispensary, so be sure to document any founders or board positions right off the bat. You don't want to have anyone feel that they were taken advantage of or led on down the road.

There a growing number of consultants specializing in the cannabis industry. Weigh your alternatives; you want to be sure that the company is qualified, and keep in mind that this option will likely be pricy.

Create bonds within the MMJ community

Have discussions with other collectives and create a coalition in the community. The more people you have working together, the greater your organization will become. You can never have too much knowledge, and new perspectives can be very helpful.

Gathering a Team

It's best not to go at this venture alone; your likelihood of success will be much greater if you can put together a team of qualified individuals. You probably already have a group of friends or associates who would help you create this entity. Remember, you can always start small and bring on new management members as needed.

The size of your collective will also determine how much assistance you will require. Keep in mind that many cities require background checks (often fingerprinting) for anyone involved with a collective, and, in general, individuals with felony convictions won't be allowed to work in (or open) a collective. Be sure you verify your particular circumstances with your local government.

Local Politics

The location of your collective will have a lot to do with how you operate. Some cities are much more liberal and accepting of collective dispensaries. You will need to do your research to determine how your local politicians feel about medical marijuana. In some instances, it may be best to befriend the mayor, a few city council members, and even some local police. On the other hand, in some instances, it is better to keep your beliefs to yourself. By attending city council and other local government meetings, you should be able to determine which side people will lean toward with regard to medical marijuana. You are better off solidifying relationships with pro-medical marijuana politicians than attempting to convert the others. Attending these meetings will also keep you active and up to date with your local government issues. In some cities, you will be fighting an uphill battle, and your only option will be to create a clandestine delivery-style collective. Nothing is foolproof, but having the right contacts can provide you with a greater sense of security.

Community Support

In order to create a successful organization, you will need allies. Only a certain percentage of the population needs medical marijuana (or uses recreationally), so you will want to make friends with as many neighbors and non-patients as possible; they can support your cause. Do your part to make your environment a better, happier place. As an active medical marijuana provider or grower, you represent the larger MMJ community. We need to work toward changing the negative stereotypes that a minority has created over the years.

Hiring an Attorney

Anyone involved in a cannabis business should have a relationship with an attorney who has experience dealing with such matters. Oftentimes, attorneys will specialize or focus on either compliance or criminal defense. Some attorneys will serve both functions or will partner with another attorney who specializes in the other area. Do your research, interview a few firms, and find someone competent with whom you feel comfortable. Also, determine and negotiate fees up front so there are no complications or misunderstandings down the road.

A compliance lawyer will be needed to help draft bylaws, file incorporating documents, and create membership and grower agreements. With the help of this book, you should be able to handle all of these items yourself, but it is recommended that you seek the advice of an attorney who can better address your specific circumstances.

A criminal attorney should also be lined up in case you or a member of your collective is arrested. You need to think of the worst-case scenario and have an emergency plan in order. The plan should include having money set aside to use for bail. Ideally, you will have enough money set aside to post bail, pay for an attorney, and provide for a few months of living expenses. Oftentimes the police will seize ALL of an individual's liquid assets (with a cultivation or sales arrest), so be sure to have an emergency account or cash to be held in trust by a family member.

Nonprofits, Not-for-Profits, and 501(c)(3) Organizations

The terms 'nonprofit' and 'not-for-profit' are for the most part interchangeable. The real differences arise when an organization receives tax-exempt status and becomes a 501(c)(3). When most people think of nonprofits, they are referring to 501(c)(3) tax-exempt organizations that derive the bulk of their funding through charitable contributions.

For example, the budgets of the American Cancer Society, Operation Smile, and the Catholic Church down the street come through contributions. These 501(c)(3) organizations are tax-exempt nonprofit corporations, or associations, that meet specific criteria and apply for exemption with the IRS.

There are various types of tax-exempt organizations recognized by the IRS (with 501(c)(3) being the most common). There is no legal distinction between nonprofit and not-for-profit; both can qualify as a tax-exempt organization under the U.S. Tax Code. The difference between tax-exempt and non-tax-exempt is the organization's business model and sources of operating funds.

A medical marijuana collective typically does not qualify as a 501(c)(3) tax-exempt organization and should not seek that status. 501(c)(3)s have more complicated tax and regulatory requirements that would be difficult to comply with. However, a properly run collective won't owe taxes, since it doesn't make a profit (and runs at a break-even or slight deficit). **Again, the 501(c)(3) federal designation isn't advised for medical marijuana entities.**

A nonprofit or not-for-profit collective derives its funding from operating a business. It provides a service—in this case, producing and providing herbal medicine—as a 'charity' and charges just enough to cover operating expenses. Very commonly, these businesses offer clients a sliding scale with those less able to pay being charged less than cost and those able to pay more making up the difference. You can also vary the cost to members based on the number of members using the service (i.e., prices go down as membership goes up).

The main issue for both types of not-for-profit entities is that no profits or dividends may leave the organization. If the entity makes a profit during any period (realistically, one year), then this excess must return to members or be put back into the organization (such as by capital improvements or charitable donations based on the will of the members).

The best way to determine this would be by vote. As long as management/officers' wages remain 'reasonable,' the board can increase them. Be sure you document the rationale for any raises and bonuses given, and please pay special attention to this.

Keep in mind that your local ordinances might restrict the use of bonuses. For example, a CA city ordinance #5526 states, "The payment of a bonus shall not be considered reasonable compensation." Because of this, bonuses are not allowed.

Incorporating/Creating your Entity

Forming an entity or incorporating in most states is done through the local office of the Secretary of State. The forms should be available online. Although these instructions vary slightly by state and entity type, the basic steps will be very similar.

1. Choose a name for your Corporation or LLC.
   a. Verify that the name you want is available (not already taken) by searching the secretary of state's website.
   b. If you are forming a Collective, you are typically aren't required to use "collective" in the name. For instance, Green Mountain Collective can be just "Green Mountain" because it *is* a collective. Not using the word "collective" will possibly help keep your organization off the radar, to some degree (based on the state you reside), and should be considered.
2. Business Details Required.
   a. What is the business address?
   b. Who will be the corporation's agent for service? An agent for service of process is the individual designated by a corporation or limited liability company to accept tax notifications and legal papers for the business. The agent must be located in the state you are registering. The agent is required to deliver documents to the owners of the business promptly. This can be a board member, attorney, or other responsible party.
   c. If necessary, choose who will be on the original board of directors (BOD).
3. File your Articles of Incorporation or Organization.
   a. This is a simple, one-page information sheet that must be typed. The main purpose of this is to

acknowledge the fundamental identifying and operating characteristics of your organization.

b. Very specific wording may be required by your state. Often the wording is vague and does not need to specifically address the business you are creating. For example, "This Corporation is a nonprofit mutual benefit corporation organized under the Nonprofit Mutual Benefit Corporation Law. The purpose of this corporation is to engage in any lawful act or activity, other than credit union business, for which a corporation may be organized under such law." Note that the main wording is about engaging in any lawful activity allowed by the state.

c. You may be required to state: "The specific purpose of this corporation is to _____."

    i. "Provide members with natural health products."

    ii. "Provide alternative forms of medicine."

    iii. "Meet the holistic medical needs of its members."

d. This statement provides the specific purpose of the entity. This statement can be brief and left very broad. Be creative; this is the organization's opportunity to highlight alternative services offered by your collective (which could be very beneficial to avoid IRS Section 280 issues, which we will discuss in Chapter 8).

e. You can find your state forms and examples online.

4. Create bylaws for your corporation or LLC Operating Agreement.

a. Bylaws (and Operating Agreements) are the rules that outline the operations of the organization and set out the form, manner, or procedure in which the organization is to be run. A corporation's founders or directors under the authority of its Articles draft these documents.

b. These documents will provide the detailed rules of the entity. It should incorporate many of the ideas that were developed in the planning process. The bylaws/operating agreement needs to comply with state law and contain the rules and procedures your entity will follow for holding meetings, how disputes are handled, electing officers and directors (if applicable), and taking care of other formalities required in your state. The more detail in these, the better. These documents form the core legal structure for your organization.

c. For not-for-profits, it is best that the board of directors be voted on by the members. You want the members to choose the oversight committee (BOD), as this is a democratic entity. Think of a collective in the traditional sense of the word, where decisions should ultimately be made to benefit the majority of the members.

5. Hold your first official board of directors meeting. (For Corporate Entities only)

Be sure that you have written minutes documenting all items discussed; the secretary of your organization should sign and date all minutes.

a. Approve the bylaws.

b. Appoint the officers who will run day-to-day operations.

c. Verify the accounting period (e.g., January 1st through December 31st).

d. Acknowledge that the corporation can begin operating.

e. Set up a corporate binder that will hold all of the recently created legal documents. All items (e.g., minutes) should be filed and kept onsite.

Corporate Compliance

As the founder of a corporation, you are required to hold meetings for your members and directors, maintain corporate records, and document major corporate decisions. If you neglect these formalities and your collective runs into legal trouble, a court may decide to disregard your corporate status and hold you personally responsible for the collective's debts or even disallow your medical exception for marijuana.

The corporation/collective is required to have a formal annual members' meeting as outlined in the bylaws. It is recommended that the collective hold member meetings more often (i.e., quarterly) to stay in closer contact with the members. A meeting can be held at any time throughout the year as long as members are given proper notice. All BOD meetings should be documented and stored in the collective's corporate binder. An example of items that would be voted on at the annual members' meeting would be:

1) Removing a director without cause
2) Filling vacancies on the board
3) Amending the bylaws or Articles of Incorporation
4) Electing to make a large capital/asset purchase

As mentioned before, LLCs typically have fewer compliance requirements than a Corporation. This is one of the benefits that should be taken into account when making your entity selection.

Annual Filing/Statement of Information

- **Corporations, LLCs, Domestic nonprofits, credit unions, and consumer cooperative corporations** may need to file a report with the secretary of state within 90 days after the filing of the initial Articles of Incorporation/LLC organization, and annual or bi-annual thereafter.

- Some states may not require this step, so be sure to visit your secretary of state's website.
- The purpose of the form is to provide the state with current information on the entity (i.e., location and management details).
- For corporations, it typically requests info about the three officer positions within the corporation: chief executive officer (CEO), chief financial officer (CFO), and secretary (your state's regulations may differ). Note that in the Incorporating section #4 above that an individual can hold all of the officer positions, if this is allowed by the bylaws.
    a) Holding all three positions is not recommended for not-for-profit entities, especially if there isn't a separate board of directors overseeing operations.
- Failure to file this form may result in a fine.

Remember that these are just general guidelines. Please visit your secretary of state's website for more specific information.

Obtaining an Employee Identification Number (EIN)

This is a federal identification number that is different from a state-issued ID number obtained from the secretary of state upon incorporation. The EIN is yours permanently and can be used immediately for most business needs, including opening a bank account, applying for business licenses, and filing a tax return by mail. However, no matter how you apply (phone, fax, mail, or online), it will take up to two weeks before your EIN becomes part of the IRS' permanent records. You must wait until this occurs before you can file an electronic return, make an electronic payment, or pass an IRS Taxpayer Identification Number matching program.

- An EIN can be obtained by phone, online or by mail.
- Taxpayers can obtain an EIN immediately by calling the Business & Specialty Tax Line at (800) 829-4933. The

hours of operation are 7:00 a.m. to 10:00 p.m. local time, Monday through Friday.

- Online is the recommended method; their website is www.irs.gov.

Chapter 4: Opening a Storefront Dispensary or Cultivation Facility

After the formation and legal matters discussed above are in place, you can turn your attention to the financial and operational aspects of your business. Many of the fundamental aspects of this chapter will also apply to the delivery service model.

Creating a Budget

Brainstorm about all potential expenses you expect the organization to have. If you have been involved with your own business before, you should have a good idea of the general business expenses that will be required.

Spreadsheet software such as Microsoft Excel, LibreOffice, or OpenOffice will help you keep your budget flexible so you can periodically make changes as more information becomes available.

You will require start-up capital. Ideally, the business will have enough cash/funding available to pay for:

- Layout design, building changes/tenant improvements required for the dispensary location, furniture, security systems, computers, reinforced doors, bulletproof glass, etc.
- Attorney/consulting fees or retainer.
- Cash reserves to cover expenses for a few months of operation (see below). This cash reserve (or available line of credit) will help you sleep much easier at night.

Funding can be a major factor in keeping people from starting any venture. It is possible to open up with a shoestring budget, but thinking ahead and involving people who can offer back-up funding is never a waste of time. Unexpected problems are inevitable, so it is always better to have access to back-up funding.

Sales projections

For sales forecasts, you can estimate the average number of patients/customers you plan to see per day and average the purchase per patient. For example, 30 patients per day, with an average purchase of one-eighth at $40 is 30 x $40 = $1,200 a day (or $1,200 x 30 days = $36,000 in revenue or reimbursement per month). For a wholesale provider, you will need to determine how often you will be harvesting and project demand from retailers.

Refer back to the Washington state examples highlighted on www.502data.com/retailers (found in the Overview of this book). Examining this information (past data, trends, current data, etc.) can help justify your sales projections. Of course, factors such as location, store size, local demographics/population, and a whole host of others will determine the final figures you achieve, but comparing your potential business to one in a similar environment (e.g., city size, population, and the like) can give you a good idea about your potential. Are you located in city comparable in size to Seattle? Sort the list by city and examine the range of numbers for a good idea of what to expect. You might also examine the individual store data that the website provides to get a more accurate picture of what's going on. You should research existing companies' websites. What strains and products are they promoting most, and at what price points? What appears to be working for them? Research never hurt anyone and, more often than not, can help the situation dramatically. Do your due diligence and you can create sales projections that are fairly accurate.

Fixed vs. variable expenses

There are two types of expenses, or costs, in any business. Fixed expenses do not fluctuate with your volume of trade. Variable expenses do.

Fixed costs include (but are not limited to):

- Rent
- Insurance
- Wages
- Leases
- Security
- Depreciation

Variable costs include (but are not limited to):

- COGS
- Packaging
- Advertising
- Shipping
- Energy usage
- Commissions

COGS (Cost of Goods Sold)

This is the cost involved in producing the medicine. Estimate your COGS as a percentage of sales. For example, COGS at 40% sales would leave 60% of sales going to cover the other operating expenses.

Example: If you charge $100 for a ¼ ounce, $40 will go towards growing the product and $60 would go towards covering all other expenses. (See Excel Spreadsheet – Attachment 1)

Note: In the case of a collective, the medicine may come from two sources: 1) The collective produces its own product. 2) Members can grow medicine and sell/seek reimbursement from the collective.

In some states, retail dispensaries cannot grow their own product and must purchase from a wholesale provider.

Operating Expenses

Operating expenses are costs associated with doing business. They cover a wide range of topics. Operating expenses are covered in more detail in Chapter 8 but may typically include:

- Rent
- Utilities
- Electricity, water, trash, Internet, alarm
- Service providers for your account
- Employees
- Payroll tax (See Chapter 9)
- Workers Compensation Insurance
- Member volunteers
- Business Insurance
- Advertising
- Supplies

Without overdoing it and turning this into accounting 101, a typical budget is usually in the following format:

Sales

Less COGS

= Gross Profit (Sales less COGS)

Less Fixed Expenses (by type)

Less Variable Expenses (by type)

= Net Profit (Gross less Total Expenses)

To chase profits at the operational level, the three issues to manage are sales, COGS, and variable expenses. At a more strategic level, you continuously try to massage your fixed costs down.

Sales Taxes: Don't forget to account for sales taxes. You either need to remove sales taxes from your gross revenue or take it out as an expense. Forgetting to account for sales taxes would create a major problem with your budget.

Choosing the Best Place for a Storefront Dispensary

The location for your medical marijuana store could be the single most important decision you ever make. Jeff Bezos, entrepreneur-investor who founded Amazon.com said that *"real estate is the key cost of physical retailers. That's why there's the old saw: location, location, location."* Better locations typically cost more but yield more income. The key is to investigate a number of options and then choose the one that will suit your needs the best.

Choosing a physical location involves four main factors:

- City Zoning – Where the town allows businesses to operate.
- City Licensing – What you have to do to get permission.
- Business Climate – The extent of local competition.
- Local Culture – The attitude of the local community to MMJ.

Let's take a quick look at how these things work in principle, remembering that this book is generalized for a nationwide audience. Be sure to check specific details about the area in which you would like to operate.

City Zoning

City planners lay out the urban area in land usage blocks that include residential (with places within them for shopping centers, schools, and churches), light industrial, medium industrial, heavy industrial, and zones for business activities. This latter zone is the one in which we are interested.

In the case of marijuana dispensaries, many cities insist that they are located at least 1,000 feet from schools, churches, parks, or other dispensaries (along similar lines to "adult only" establishments).

Visit your city planning office and ask to see the zoning map. You will find the business sections have sub-classifications for different purposes such as commercial, retail, etc. Ask how an MMJ storefront fits into this mix so you can identify where your options are. You may find an opportunity in an "unincorporated" area (outside city limits) where the zoning defaults to general state and/or county laws.

If you are planning to rent existing space without structural alterations, then you can probably stop at this point. On the other hand, if you are planning to construct new facilities, then you'll need to investigate building regulations including possible restrictions, coverage, maximum height, permit fees, parking, etc. Make notes of the key information and get the name of the administrator you spoke with in case you need to follow up.

City Licensing

Most businesses need some type of license so the various agencies can track them and tax them accordingly. As a rule of thumb, if you are anywhere in the medical marijuana supply chain, then the chances are you need one. To get an overview, ask the city authorities or visit the NORML website for the latest news regarding your state.

The best advice that we can give is to follow these requirements to the letter. Sadly, some with power to prosecute/close you down are still clinging to 'the old ways' and could make the licensing process miserable. But once you get your head around what you need to do, you will find most of the requirements spelled out in the application documents.

You are going to have to apply for and obtain several different permits to do business; some at the city level, some at the state level, and some at the federal level.

Please make sure to research the following:

- Business Licensing (where you pay application and/or annual renewal fees): The process normally includes zone-use permit, background check, property deed or rental agreement, and approval of the premises.
- Occupational Licenses (where the application and/or annual renewal fees are due for all employees working anywhere in the supply chain): Applicants must typically be age twenty-one or older, not have related undischarged felony convictions, and be a resident of the state at the time of application.
- Registration for federal and state payroll taxes, city property taxes, and state and sometimes city sales taxes. In some cities you will find additional sales taxes applied to marijuana sales. This extra income is the incentive to a lot of government agencies.

Business Climate

In a perfect world, you would be the sole MJ provider in the area. While you may be lucky enough to find such a spot, the chances are good that as you prosper, you will draw in competition. However, we don't recommend that you shy away from competition. In fact, operating where there is other like business reinforces the fact that demand exists and the community is accepting.

You should consider the following criteria to make an informed decision:

- How supportive are the city administration and local population of new businesses and MJ business in particular? Is there a moratorium on medical marijuana dispensaries in place? Are they open minded about these facilities, or do they have a "not in my backyard" mindset?
- How helpful is the local Chamber of Commerce? Are they open to MMJ, or are they too conservative? Do

they proactively introduce you to potential mentors and related businesses?

- What responses did you get from the city administration when you mentioned plans to open a marijuana dispensary? Were they enthusiastic, or did they go cold?

- As you narrow down your choice locations, ask a few friends to inspect them with you. If your location of choice is a fixer-upper, create an estimated budget to get up and running.

- Ideally, your location will have great sidewalk appeal to draw in customers. What is the general standard of nearby commercial buildings? How good is the city at removing garbage and filling potholes?

- Will customers find you easily? Will zoning and the community allow you to put up adequate signage? How safe is the neighborhood during business hours? Where can customers park?

These things all matter. Preferably, you want to be part of a community/neighborhood that is on the up and up. You typically don't want your medical marijuana dispensary located in a run-down part of town, as that could discredit your operation and contribute to a negative stereotype.

Local Culture

People like to follow causes. The last things you want are chanting protestors up and down the street and negative media. We recommend researching how the community voted on previous marijuana issues. If everything checks out, then you made it through the starting blocks. The next thing to consider is finding an ideal facility for your operation.

Choosing the Best Place for a Cultivation/Processing Facility

The major difference between choosing a site for a cultivation/processing facility and a dispensary is that the latter needs a prominent retail (more urban) location, while cultivation is best suited in a commercial or agriculture area. Indoor cultivations often thrive out of sight in low-rent districts.

Please read this section in conjunction with the previous one about choosing the best place for a dispensary, as we only highlight the differences here.

Federal, State, and City Restrictions

- Visit the local municipality and ask about the guidelines for opening/operating a cultivation facility. Find out what similar businesses already exist or are in the approval phase. There may be proximity restrictions that rule out some areas. Enquire about applicable constraints while you are there.
- Factor in the need to be at least 1,000 feet away from public or private schools, universities, places of worship, and daycare centers. In fact, while the federal government keeps playing hardball, stay that distance from any government building. Don't even imagine that 999 feet is good enough.

What's Best: Combination Sites or Separate Sites?

If you are growing, processing, and dispensing, then you may want everything on a single site. However, zoning restrictions often prevent this. It's not that the city is necessarily prejudice against marijuana; it's that they have certain areas for certain activities like operations (i.e., farming, manufacturing, or retail). The alternative is to base yourself in a rural area where planning is more informal or split your operations.

Combination sites can be cost effective because there is no traveling or shipping required and you can get away with fewer personnel when they multi-task. It is also easier to secure a single site. Another advantage to the combination site is that you can remain close to, and "hands-on" with, your sensitive crops.

Unlike a city area, though, semi-rural locations do not necessarily have sufficient utilities for what you want to do. Check out the following:

- Is there sufficient electricity available?
- Do you have adequate water for a thirsty business?
- Does the brown water drainage have the capacity to cope?
- What is the state of the HVAC? Is the facility insulated?
- Research neighboring business, and anticipate potential conflicts.

Cash flow is especially delicate during the start-up phase before you begin generating income. Anticipate outflows in advance and have a budget to address them.

Have an operating license before you commit to a rental agreement (or at least a cancellation clause in case your license application fails).

Security & Dispensary Floor Plan

Security Measures

Dispensaries should have the functionality of a bank with the feel of a medical facility. With a secure, well-run dispensary, there shouldn't be a need for guards because you secured the dispensary with the items outlined below. Your aim is to avoid problems with preventive measures - with proper procedures in place, you can.

- **Cameras** – An averaged-sized (1,000–1,500 sq. ft.) dispensary should have a system of eight to ten cameras placed strategically throughout the installation. Appropriate systems are available online at Amazon or eBay for around $500. Make sure the video has record/DVR back up for at least two weeks and is stored in a locked or discreet location.

  Make a habit of testing the system frequently; the last thing you want is to have an incident occur and not get it on tape. Backing up the videos off-site in the cloud is ideal.

- **Alarm system** – You will want to install a 24-hour security system that will detect any break-ins at the location using a combination of glass breakage sensors and motion detectors. A company like ADT should be sufficient and will be able to consult with you on various options.

  When an alarm signal triggers, the security company will call the dispensary's first point of contact (e.g., the manager). If there is no answer to the first call—or if the first contact suspects a break in—the security company will then call the police.

- **Electronic door** – This provides a measure of security so that strangers can't just walk in while allowing employees to buzz in patients without needing to get up from the desk. Make sure they have video or line of sight to the far side of the door before they trigger the release.

- **Security glass** – Depending on your location and security needs, you many want security glass at your first point of entry. If done properly, you can still provide an inviting feel to the dispensary. If security is priority number one, then you will want to go this route. Dispensaries often have high volumes of cash and marijuana on hand, which will entice criminals. Get high-quality security glass (similar to what you find at a bank or convenience store) with a paper slot at the bottom. These are available for around $1,000 online.

Waiting room

This is where patients and non-patients await assistance, fill out paperwork, and receive their orders. This room provides the first impression for the dispensary, so keep it clean, professional looking, and tidy at all times.

In addition, have some medical marijuana information available. Americans for Safe Access sells a series of handbooks (at a reasonable price) that provide information on cannabis usage to treat various health issues. These make for excellent reading material.

Do not set out samples or other live medical products, as this is typically prohibited.

Restroom

A neat and clean restroom is essential for employees and patients alike. Both personal preference and city ordinances come into play here, but maintain some form of access control and inspect the facility hourly to ensure it maintains the image of your brand.

Dispensing Area / Green Room

For security, and to utilize space efficiently, you will probably want to have a limited quantity of each strain available in the retail green room. Two to three ounces of each should be sufficient. This will serve as your active inventory from which you take grams and smaller quantities.

- **Menu Board** – Your dispensary will need a menu board(s) that is easy to modify as strains change on a daily basis.
  - o Medicine comes in grams, ⅛ ounce, ¼ ounce, ½ ounce, or 1 ounce.
  - o Concentrates typically sell in portions of ½ grams or grams.
  - o Shake, pre-rolls/joints, and edibles are also products that you may have available.

Depending on the size of the board and the extent of your product range, you can either list everything on the main menu board or have sets of supplementary ones. Here, again, you have options depending on your budget and the character of your brand:

  - o An LCD flat screen TV that changes as you update your stock
  - o A static board (this can be a pain to update in a hurry)
  - o A chalk or dry erase board to which you will add items manually
- **Storage Containers** – Storage containers can be glass or plastic; just make sure that they are airtight to keep the medicine fresh. Glass mason jars with pull-down clips work well, but they don't stack nicely and can take up a lot of space. Some high-quality plastic 'Tupperware' products also do the trick.
- **Samples** – The green room should have samples of all the strains for the patients to see. Typically, you will have one nice-sized flower/bud of each strain in a small jar for patients to review. Although not required, it is nice to allow the patients to touch and smell the product. This lets them get the best sense of the quality (short of smoking it).
- **Shake** – You should also have a decent amount of shake. This is the small, loose pieces of bud naturally

created from day-to-day operations. Shake can be sold as-is for smoking and cooking, but the dispensary will be able to shift a lot more if it's pre-rolled and ready to smoke.

A good, basic pre-roll will contain between 0.8 and 1 grams of shake. The best idea is to keep the A+ (Kush) shake separate from your average shake. This will allow the collective to recoup more (i.e., $8 versus $5) for the grade-A pre-roll. It's a good idea to ask growers to donate shake to the collective...or at least to provide it at a significant discount.

Consider having employees roll a set number of pre-rolls every day or week that will be available for purchase (if applicable). If a procedure isn't put in place, it is highly unlikely that this will happen consistently. If allowable, you should have shake available for sale. Consistent sales of pre-rolls and shake will help the dispensary cover its expenses and keep patients happy. You may even consider asking to "add-on" special pre-rolls with every purchase at a given price.

Legal Considerations/Requirements (MEDICAL MARIJUANA ONLY)

Make sure to verify with your local regulators the maximum allowable purchase per member, per day. This will typically be between 2 and 8 ounces. Obviously then, if someone purchases a large amount of medicine, then they shouldn't be back for a while.

It would be a good idea to make notes in patients' files to ensure that they aren't buying large quantities more often than would be reasonable for personal usage. There are software programs that can assist with this process. Remember that diversion of medical marijuana to non-patients is illegal and will likely find its way back to the source. You don't want to be that source; this could jeopardize your operation and even subject you to criminal violations.

The dispensary can also run periodic or ongoing specials, but please be careful in the wording of your current specials. It doesn't look good when the dispensary appears to function as a typical retail store.

Creating an Emergency Plan

Given the gray area of our industry, you will unfortunately need to plan for multiple "emergencies" that could arise due to your involvement with medical marijuana. Following state laws and local guidelines is critical. However, you should be aware that until marijuana is legal on a federal level, there is no way to ensure that you won't face arrest or be shut down by local or federal law enforcement for one reason or another.

If you are running a dispensary/collective, then illegal activities by members could negatively affect you too. Criminals see medical marijuana cultivators and providers as easy targets, so you need to be extra cautious with everything you do. Member employees need to be aware of these potential risks before they are hired. Everybody working or volunteering onsite needs to be prepared for the situations below.

Risks to Prepare For

You (or the organization) need to have plans in place for:

- Raids by local police
- Raids by federal agents
- Robbery
- The arrest of an employee
- The arrest of someone who cultivates for you

- The arrest of a patient member (if applicable)

Think ahead and be ready for a worst-case scenario. What if your operation gets raided? Have a plan of action ready. After you assess the situation, and you consult with your attorney, are you going to re-open immediately? In some instances, the answer might be yes. Every day that your operation/dispensary is closed, more patients are going elsewhere for medicine, and they may never return. Do you have back-up product and funds available offsite? Remember that if the storefront gets raided, the authorities will likely visit the homes of all the directors and managers as well.

There should be specific plans of action for these and other potential scenarios that the management team should agree to follow. The various emergency plans would include detailed tasks and responsibilities delegated among the core team. There need to be clear, simple steps for who to contact and who is in charge of which actions.

Periodically reviewing these plans will help reduce panic during an actual event. Non–management members might also need to be involved in certain situations (i.e., what if the entire management team is detained). It is much better to be over-prepared than to be caught off-guard. This should also help you sleep better at night.

Importance of a Large Safe

Robbery is a major concern in the medical marijuana business. You need a large safe in which to store money and medicine. One large, heavy-duty gun safe should provide more than enough room. Ideally, the safe should be secured to the floor. It is best to keep the bulk of the medicine in the locked safe throughout the day so that access to the marijuana is as difficult as possible.

Preferably, you will also have a second, hidden floor safe (cemented in) to which you can periodically move money from the register(s). If you don't have a separate floor safe, keep the money locked in the large safe with the medicine. Excess cash surplus in the short term should go offsite.

Bail Fund

If such unfortunate circumstances should arrive, you will want to have the option of bailing yourself (or other directors or employees) out of jail. You will have to weigh the options of paying the money and bailing out, or spending a few nights in jail and waiting for release on your own recognizance. Bailing out means you will spend as little time in jail as possible. You will, however, be out a few thousand dollars, depending on how high the bail is set.

In California, for example, the courts typically set bail at $20,000 to $100,000. That means you would need to pay $2,000 to $10,000 for a bail bondsman. Another benefit of bailing out is that you won't have to abide by any terms of the district attorney.

When a person is released on his or her own recognizance, they often cannot reopen or associate with the dispensary, so this can end up being a complicated decision. In the end, however, it's always better to have the option be yours instead of depending on the mercy of the court.

Chapter 5: Day to Day Operations

Knowing your Medical Marijuana

Dispensary green room workers (or 'bud tenders') who distribute medical marijuana to patients should be familiar with the products they are providing. The best way to become familiar with the product is through experience. Experience can be gained by sampling the various strains. Be aware that identical strains can vary significantly given different growing conditions. Bud tenders should follow current trends and research developments in the market.

Provide samples of flowers to employees of the collective, note their feedback, and pass that information on to your members. New patients will need advice regarding the various products and potencies available. Bud tenders will need to make recommendations as to what products will best meet each patient's needs, because there are countless strains/types of marijuana that provide treatment for a great variety of medical conditions.

Medical marijuana users come in all shapes and sizes, and their medical marijuana needs can be significantly different. Along with product recommendations, you should provide dosage information to novice patients. Keep in mind that various edible products should be available for those patients who can't smoke (be sure you make the potency of those products known as well).

Be aware that you need to inspect carefully all the marijuana brought into and sold at the dispensary for risks such as mold, mildew, and pests. Unfortunately, there is dirty medicine out there, and this can come from both novice and large-scale, professional cultivators. A digital scope or jeweler's eyepiece with 30X magnification should allow you to detect a lot of these problems. Fortunately, lab testing is becoming more common and some states require that all marijuana be tested before it is sold. This is great for the patients; with these tests, a patient can feel confident that the flowers (and various products) are free from pathogenic molds and pesticides. Potency testing is also available, which provides the percentages of three major cannabinoids: THC, CBD and CBN (discussed more below).

Some physical characteristics to look for when assessing medical cannabis for quality include density, dryness, color, crystals, hairs, and hopefully, no seeds. The bud/flower will ideally be fairly fluffy with heavy crystallization and a pungent aroma. The presence of crystals—called trichomes—or resin indicates a decent level of THC. However, you will want to make sure the supplier dried the flowers properly so the weight is accurate and mold doesn't incubate.

Strains

There are three distinctly different kinds of cannabis: *Cannabis Sativa, Cannabis Indica,* and *Cannabis Ruderalis.* The common *sativa* and *indica* strains possess very different characteristics. The latter *ruderalis* is an uncommon variety that grows wild in parts of Eastern Europe and Russia. It's occasionally used in hybrids (the intentional crossing of two different genotypes of cannabis) to help the resulting plants cope better with harsh climates.

So a strain is a unique/specific type of cannabis that can have either sativa and/or indica characteristics. The current number of strains available is very difficult if not impossible to determine, but definitely thousands; Leafy.com recently listed about two thousand different strains. It's like trying to tie down how many race variations humans have. Cultivators can cross strains any number of times and create unique blends. Cultivators and dispensaries can miss-name or rename strains (accidentally or on purpose) creating more confusion. Thankfully, as you get more experience seeing (and smoking) various flowers, you will get better at identifying strains and their characteristics.

Sativa

Sativa plants are tall and thin with narrow leaves and a lighter green color. The buds are typically loosely packed and are lighter than the *indica* variety. *Sativas* grow very quickly and in extreme cases can reach heights of 20 feet in a single season. This strain originated in equatorial regions including Colombia, Mexico, Thailand, and Southeast Asia. Once a *sativa* plant begins to flower, it can take anywhere from 10 to 16 weeks to fully mature. This is much longer than the *indica* plant that will mature fully in 6-8 weeks.

The *sativa* high is cerebral, social, and energetic. *Sativa* strains are most associated with laughter, long discussions about nothing, and enhanced audio and visual senses. Super Silver Haze and Headband are two examples of the *sativa* strain. Some patients experience a specific focus on detail and can have a heightened sense of enjoyment.

Indica

Indica plants come from harsh parts of the world such as Afghanistan, Morocco, and Tibet. They are short, dense plants with broad leaves, and they are often a darker green. *Indica* buds are thick and dense with flavors and aromas ranging from pungent skunk to sweet and fruity. The *indica* high is generally a 'body type' of high that yields relaxing and mellow sensations. This is the best type of cannabis for easing pain or helping a patient fall asleep. Two typical *indica* strains are OG Kush and Grand Daddy Purple.

Cross Strains/Hybrids

A good *indica/sativa* cross can give patients the best of both worlds. Cross breeding these plants creates hybrids containing the desirable characteristics of both strains. Breeders work hard to develop varieties that provide a well-balanced head high matched with a relaxing body sensation. Hybrids can be more dominant *sativa* or *indica* depending on the specific strains crossed and characteristics of the phenotypes used.

Active ingredients: (Cannabinoids)

There are more than 80 identified cannabinoids in the cannabis plant, and every strain has its own particular genetic combination. The active cannabinoids each have unique physiological effects, and many combinations appear to have synergistic and antagonistic effects as well. The following are the most common natural herbal cannabinoids found in cannabis THC (long form delta-9-tetrahydrocannabinol):

- Cannabidiol (CBD):

  Lessens the psychoactive effects of THC and has sedative and analgesic effects.

- Cannabichromene (CBC):

  Promotes the effects of THC and has sedative and analgesic effects.

- Cannabigerol (CBG):

  Has sedative effects and anti-microbial properties as well as lowering intra-ocular pressure. CBG is the biogenetic precursor of all other cannabinoids.

- Cannabinol (CBN):

  Is a mildly psychoactive degradation of THC. Its primary benefits are reducing inflammation, anti-pain, anti-epileptic and helping patients sleep.

Each individual strain of cannabis will have different amounts of these various cannabinoids.

Pricing Medical Marijuana

As a business, you will need to experiment to find a price point that best suits your needs. You need to take the following items into account.

- The cost of the product.
- What are competitors charging?
- Are sales greatly affected if you increase (or decrease) product prices?
  - o This will likely depend on the quality of the product and how easily a substitute can be obtained.
- Keep in mind that you want your customers to feel that you are providing them with a fair value and not trying to squeeze as much money out of them as possible.

As a starting point, a dispensary needs to determine its break-even cost (per transaction), an amount to cover the cost to produce the product and an allocation towards overhead expenses. There are various ways to do this, but the best way is to estimate the monthly sales and monthly overhead expenses and add a percentage on top of the product costs (for each sale) for overhead expenses. In doing this, each sale will contribute toward the operating expenses of the collective. Please keep in mind that there are other ways to calculate, but the end result should be the same.

Examples:

Assumptions:

1) The dispensary estimates selling about 2 ounces a day for the month while being open 6 days a week (24 days

x 2 ounces) = 3 pounds per month (1 pound converts to 453.59 grams, rounded to 450 grams per pound).

2) Average cost to the dispensary for a pound of marijuana is $2,000. So we estimate the total monthly product cost/COGS to be $6,000 (or 3 pounds x $2,000).

3) Assume estimated monthly operating expenses of the dispensary are $8,000 (payroll, rent, utilities, etc.).

4) Given these assumptions, our operating expenses are roughly **133%** of the cost of our product ($8,000/$6,000 = 1.333). So if our estimates were right on, our break-even point would be 3 pounds for $6,000 x 2.33 = $13,980, which would cover our product COGS and operating expenses (less $20 lost to rounding). The 2.33 multiplier is the 1.33 for operating expenses + 1.00 for the product.

Please note/take into consideration that the "operating expenses" (from #3 above) could also include compensation to the owners (or investors), which could affect this amount significantly.

Example 1 – Determining the selling price of a specific strain:

The dispensary buys one pound (lb.) of Sour Diesel for $2,200 (including all expenses and labor at a reasonable rate per hour). The cost per gram would be roughly $4.89 ($2,200/450). This is our base price. Now we add our overhead costs estimated at 133% of the product cost (per #4 above), so our break-even price per gram to charge members would be $4.89 x 2.33 or $11.39. So we could charge let's say $15/gram and be making about 30% profit.

Example 2 – Determining the selling price of a specific strain:

The dispensary buys one pound of outdoor OG Kush for $1,200 (including all expenses and labor at a reasonable rate per hour). The price per gram would be roughly $2.67 ($1,200/450). This is our base price. Now we add our overhead costs estimated at 133% of the product cost, so our break-even price per gram to charge members would be $2.67 x 2.33 or $6.22.

Your equations will need to be adjusted at least monthly, as your estimates will change based on actual results (and new forecasts). Keep in mind that you can add a cushion into your overhead percentage for any emergency funds or other items that the collective feels are appropriate.

In most industries, consumers are given a discount for buying in bulk. This should remain true for both not-for-profits and traditional businesses. If a patient buys in bulk, then he or she should pay less overhead, as they will visit the collective fewer times per month and will use fewer resources. You can add these assumptions into your calculations.

Example 3 – Reduced break-even pricing for larger purchases:

- ⅛th ounce is 3.5 grams with a 10% reduction in overhead allowance
- 120% instead of 133% = $5.87/gram ($2.67 x 2.20) based on Example #2
- ⅛th price = $20.55 ($5.87 x 3.5 gram)

Make sure you document all your assumptions and monitor your finances often to make sure the dispensary is pricing the medicine correctly.

Sales Tax (or other Marijuana tax)

You can either add sales tax on top of the sale price or include it in the price to keep the numbers rounded.

Option a: $10 gram with 8% sales tax ($0.80) added would be $10.80 total.

Option b: Charge $11 flat, which is the $10.19/gram base price and $.815 tax (rounded). This would keep your cash and change transactions simpler but may complicate your internal accounting.

Option b(2): Determine the final price (with tax) that you wish to charge and work backwards to find the sales amount before tax.

Equation: Final price = x + (sales tax*x)

11 = x + (.08x). NOTE: The x all by itself can be thought of as "1x". That makes the addition easier: 1x + 0.08x = 1.08x

11/1.08x

So X = $10.19 per gram pretax

Metric to American-Standard Weight Conversion

3.5 grams = ⅛ ounce

7 grams = ¼ ounce

14 grams = ½ ounce

28 grams = 1 ounce

454 grams = 1 pound

All ratios have been rounded.

A not-for-profit entity is established to provide qualified patients with marijuana for medical needs. <u>Ultimately, the not-for-profit should not have a profit at year end (money left over after all expenses have been paid).</u> If surplus income is left over, then it is up to the board or members to decide how best to utilize this. A few possibilities are to make capital purchases or improvements (e.g., buy a van for collective operations and to transport members, provide members with cash back or free product, or donate the money to charity).

<u>Inventory Controls</u>

Medical marijuana is a very valuable and sought-after product. You will need solid procedures in place to guarantee that the dispensary's medicine is not being misappropriated (stolen). This will require frequent physical counts of the inventory as well as an accurate accounting of sales. We have attached a manual spreadsheet (**Attachment #2**) that you can use as a reference or template. Ideally, your point-of-sale (POS) or Seed to Sale system will track inventory, and you will need to know what the current inventory is at any given time. A variance report (inventory system vs. actual) will need to be created. [Note: If you have properly implemented a "Seed to Sale" system, then your inventory should be properly recorded; this will decrease the chances of products being sidetracked (or lost). However, you still want to use prudence and constantly consider if there are leaks in your internal control process.]

If your green room and sales register employee switch shifts mid-day, then you will want to crosscheck by performing a count then as well. You might encounter an instance where one strain is a few grams short but another strain is a few grams over. That would most likely indicate that the wrong product was run through the computer system.

You need to be more concerned with the overall variance. The variance report is a great control to have in place and should deter employees from trying to misappropriate product. In addition, you will definitely want to make sure that only your manager can adjust your POS. Also, any adjustment or product removed from the system should be recorded and kept on file. If your employees are changing each day, then a recount should be done in the morning to verify the existing inventory.

This makes every worker accountable for his or her sales and inventory counts. Management should constantly be looking for holes in the system and correcting any that are found.

Depending on the quality of your medicine, a certain percentage will turn to shake. This should be kept in a daily shake jar and added to the totals to reconcile for the day. This shouldn't create a problem in general, but please be aware that there is a potential for small misappropriations of "good" product that are then substituted for by old shake.

If you don't have a POS system in place, then you can create the same procedure manually. You will need to track and add all your daily activity. Create a "tally sheet" with the various strains that can be quickly marked off each time a sale takes place. At the end of the day, total the sales per strain and remove that amount from your beginning inventory. See **Attachment 2** for an example. At the end of each day, your calculated inventory should match your actual inventory. Microsoft Excel or Open Office software will make the accounting much easier.

If your volume picks up, you may want to streamline your inventory process by having pre-weighed packages (e.g., 2 ounces total, pre-weighed into one ¼ ounce, eight ⅛ths, and 21 grams) that you can move from the safe to the floor easily. You will typically want to have smaller quantities to work with in the green room. You don't want to be picking grams out of your larger (¼ pound+) bags, which will deteriorate the product over time. If someone wants a larger quantity, you can take that directly from the safe without affecting the green room inventory. This format will also make the daily inventory counting simpler.

Another way to simplify things is to always keep the same units (e.g., 1 pound or 2 oz. bags) in the safe and smaller units in the green room. You should keep a separate listing of the safe inventory, and that should be updated when products are moved.

Receipts

Retain a copy of the receipts from each day's sales. If you have a computer-based point-of-sales system, saving an external electronic backup is sufficient. If you are using carbon-copy paper receipts, staple daily sales together and take them to storage. You will need to retain these for a minimum of three years, and they will be needed if you are subject to a financial audit. To be cautious, it is probably best to keep the bulk of your receipts and financial records at a secure location offsite.

Tracking Your Marijuana from Seed to Sale

As marijuana becomes more accepted, many states are taxing the sales and closely watching the production cycle though "seed-to-sale" tracking. This tracking system typically applies an ID number to a seed and related child numbers to flowers and trim produced by the original seed. Cultivators and dispensaries use this system to comply with state regulations. This tracking process typically revolves around bar codes or Radio Frequency Identification (RFID) tags. These RFID tags enable industry-wide end-to-end tracking from seed through the grow cycle and to the final dried flowers for retail sale. Plant tags typically have the licensee's name, ID number, date, and plant ID number. This allows the plants and flowers to be easily identified, tracked, and audited onsite or remotely.

With these types of software, entities can easily identify where and when a product was produced through the point of sale. The government requires these systems to provide transparency and accountability. The goal of the agencies overseeing is to ensure that the cannabis does not deviate from its intended purpose and can be monitored and taxed appropriately.

The software is not only for compliance but typically facilitates with the cultivation process, tracks patient purchases, and integrates with accounting programs (i.e., QuickBooks), so you can have consistent data seamlessly. These software programs take time and money to implement, but business owners can often benefit from the security and information provided. Operations that are familiar with the software are much better prepared if/when tracking becomes mandatory in their state. If you're just starting an MMJ business, consider at least testing a tracking system. If you're an existing MMJ business where tracking is not required, anticipate it and be ready to make the transition.

Agrisoft, BioTrackTHC and METRC or "Marijuana Enforcement Tracking Reporting Compliance" are currently the large players in the seed-to-sale software space. BioTrackTHC currently has state contracts with Washington, New Mexico, Illinois, New York, and Hawaii. METRC currently has contracts with Alaska, Oregon, and Colorado.

The companies behind these programs are constantly bettering themselves and the technology is always improving. Over and above the obvious benefits of complying with the law, it is good businesswise to have real-time details of your inventory (and cultivation status).

So What Makes Marijuana Seed-to-Sale software special?

These solutions are created specifically for this industry and track the entire marijuana supply chain from the cultivator to wholesaler to supplier to beneficiary. A number of medical and recreational dispensaries, cultivators, and state governments use it. The software has the ability to tag and track cannabis plants from seedling to the consumer, either in flower form or further processed as a concentrate or edible. Even the waste is traceable with these systems.

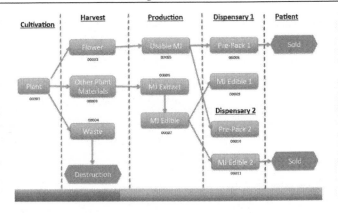

BioTrackTHC incorporates an anonymous customer tracking system using fingerprints and DNA to prevent patients 'gaming the system' to obtain more product at different doctors' offices and dispensaries.

In the case of BioTrackTHC, the developer was originally operating a chain of medical centers in Fort Lauderdale, Florida, and saw the need to identify out-of-state patients coming in to ask for prescriptions for traditional schedule drugs. Their goal was to create a legitimate software solution. They did, and this product evolved and carried over into the MMJ space. They currently have over 1,700 dispensaries and cultivators as customers who are happy with their product.

There are other creditable cannabis tracking software providers (besides Agrisoft, BiotrackTHC and METRC); check out MJFreeway.com, Adilas, Flowhub.co or ViridianSciences.com for more info.

Bank Accounts

As you would imagine, it is easier to run a business with a bank account for a number of reasons; a bank account allows you a safe place to store your earnings, write checks, online bill pay, and ACH transfer. Many service providers (e.g., payroll) require that you have a bank account. There is substantial convenience and flexibility with using checks and electronic transaction. Checks provide a better trail than cash and money orders. Currently, most banks won't accept dispensary customers. However, it is still worth the effort to try to open an account. Smaller, local banks and credit unions are probably your best bet. It will help if you already have a relationship with the bank or a banker. If you can't do without a bank account, you might need to expand the services offered, amend the collective's bylaws, and develop a broader description of the operations.

To open a Corporate bank account, you will need the following: a business tax ID (EIN), Articles of Incorporation, a current statement of information, and possibly a corporate resolution defining bank signers. Usually two of the three officers of the corporation must be present. The requirements are similar for an LLC, but typically only one member is required to open an account.

Worst case scenario: As part of your overall procedures, you may determine to keep a low reserve balance in your bank account because. Unfortunately, the police or the government can seize your funds with the snap of their fingers. So it's best to keep cash reserves in a secure site away from the dispensary, such as the property of a member of the board of directors or other agreed-upon location. As expenses are due, you can make adequate deposits to cover them. To reiterate, we are not condoning any illegal activities or money laundering; you should have accurate records regardless of how funds are received or stored. Your goal is to protect the collective's assets. It is better to play it safe than to risk having all your funds seized.

We try to keep our finger on the pulse of the industry and continually seek to provide new options for the MJ entrepreneur; check our website (MMJUpdates.com) for the latest new and/or sign up for their newsletter.

Free (or discounted) medicine

Medical marijuana should be available to all people regardless of their income level. Unfortunately, the current Medicare system does not help patients obtain it. The collective should have a policy in place (approved by the board) where it will provide discounted medicine (or free) to needy individuals who can't afford it. There are many ways to go about doing this. One way is to discount your lower-end medicine in general to help those patients in need. If too many patients are claiming hardships, then you can create a lottery system and pick a given number of patients to help per week. Don't forget to be compassionate and help those in need. And remember to closely track all of the medicine that is given away. This should be incorporated into the collective's inventory control system (discussed in Chapter 5).

Accounting

Accounting is a huge part of any business, but it is extremely important to a dispensary; they deal with a lot of cash, and they are under more scrutiny (from various organizations/administrations) than other businesses. You need to weigh the pros and cons of doing it yourself versus using an outside bookkeeper or accounting firm.

If no one in your organization has a business background, you will, at a minimum, need to have someone set up your accounting system and give you instructions. Make sure the system works for you, because you won't be able to get good information out of a bad system. Fortunately, as this industry has grown, a number of companies have stepped up and create software specially for cultivators and dispensaries. The strongest companies are those that are complaint with the seed-to-sale tracking; again, we will reference BioTrack, MJ Freeway, and and Agrisoft. These companies provide training and support and should be able to help you develop a strong foundation. You will still need basic accounting knowledge to know how to classify various expenses properly.

Assess the skills of your employees and the time available for them to do your accounting work. You will need someone who is competent enough to make accurate entries and keep clean records. You will also want to have systems in place when operations get busy. It is much easier and more productive to keep your records current instead of having to go back months later and make data entries.

If you don't have an integrated seed-to sale system, then a good bookkeeper or consultant should be able to set up some accounting procedures and give you (and other employees who will be keeping records) a basic understanding of the process. This will get your organization on the right track.

The qualified consultant (or CPA) should also provide you with periodic check-ups to ensure that things are running smoothly. You can create a miscellaneous account within your accounting program for entries that you have questions about. That way these entries are easily identified for the consultant rather than being hidden throughout the financial statements.

Establishing dispensary procedures will ensure that all income and expense items are recorded every day. You will also need a procedure for collecting receipts and recording any cash payouts. Typically, you would write this information down in a ledger and file the receipts. At the end of the day, you would reconcile your income and expenses and record everything in your accounting software. Reconciling needs to be done each night to ensure that there are no unexplained discrepancies in either cash or inventory (as outlined in the Inventory control section). Ideally, entries would be made every day into the accounting system, but weekly is acceptable; just be sure you don't get too far behind. Keep in mind that the further behind you get, the harder it is to remember or track down additional information if needed.

The accounting software will allow you to run periodic profit and loss statements (known as P&L), which you can use to assess the efficiency of the business and compare to the budget (as we recommended in the Budget section, Chapter 4). This will keep management in alignment with the business and can allow for more frequent and accurate product price adjustments. These financial records will also make it easier for your tax accountant to complete the necessary filings.

Your dispensary might receive product on consignment (review the Consignment Section in Chapter 8). The dispensary will owe these cultivators money once their products are sold. You will need to track these debts, and it is probably best to do this within the accounting software, although you can keep a separate spreadsheet for this if you find that easier. These expenses need to be included in your accounting system at some point for your P&L to be accurate. Keep in mind that your overall COGS will be incorrect until all of the consignment product is sold through.

As we mentioned earlier, there are a few point-of-sale software programs that have been designed specifically for dispensaries. Since this industry is still growing rapidly, these software systems are trying to keep up and adapt to the needs of dispensaries. You want a system that seamlessly interacts with a patient database system and a robust accounting program. Typically, if you are looking for top-of-the-line programs, you will need to integrate systems (Seed-to-sale software with a robust accounting program like QuickBooks).

Many traditional businesses are moving to paperless offices where all items are scanned in and the paper copy is shredded or recycled. This paperless procedure might be very advantageous to dispensaries that want to keep a tight control on who gets access to financial data.

There are also bookkeepers who are available to work remotely. Under this setup, you fax or email your daily ledger and receipts, and they do all the data entry for you (via remote desktop or other systems like QuickBooks Online). If you are using a bank account (and/or credit cards), transaction reports can often be uploaded directly to accounting software, which makes the bookkeeping very efficient. The dispensary should produce monthly, if not weekly, profit and loss (P&L) reports.

Merchant services

In order to accept credit card payments, you will need a merchant account that typically links to your bank account. Accepting credit cards is a good option to have for your patients, and it will often increase patient purchases.

The merchant service business is highly competitive, so it pays to shop and compare. When considering a merchant service, beware of hidden fees, high percentage rates, and cancellation fees. PayPal is a potential provider worth looking into. It accepts credit card payment through smart phones and various online applications. This option will likely only qualify if the collective offers a significant portion of non-marijuana products or services.

As of mid-2016, most national U.S. banks will still not process credit card transactions for medical marijuana dispensaries. However, there are alternatives available. There are a few smaller companies that offer merchant services. These offerings continue to change as does the industry. Please visit the Resources Page on our website for the current options available.

As an alternative, some dispensaries find it convenient to have an ATM machine located in the lobby or green room.

Advertising and Marketing (Finding New Collective Members)

It is very important to know the views of your city government and law enforcement when it comes to medical or recreational marijuana advertisements. Please research your local market and keep in mind that law enforcement may be reading your ads. In certain markets/locations, placing or responding to personal ads about medical marijuana have been used to trap people.

Referrals and Word of Mouth

You most likely already know a handful of people who would like to cultivate with you or obtain product from you. The best way to round up interested parties is word of mouth, and the smaller, more tightly knit operations seem to avoid problems. Gaining word of mouth is as simple as providing high-quality medicine. Keep a friendly, clean, professional environment that you are proud of, and word of mouth referrals will come.

Also, talk with clients/patient members to see what they like and don't like about their own organizations. Encourage patients to provide you with feedback on all aspects of your operation. Put your heart into your organization, and do your best to make them happy. Medical marijuana patients often have friends and associates who are also patients. Using that network is one of the best ways to add to your membership base. Incentive medicine or discounts for referrals can be a good motivation for existing patients to help recruit new patients. At the same time, offering first-time specials to new members will increase the likelihood that they will join your collective. A broader patient base will allow for better, cheaper medicine, and everyone should be excited about that. However, please be aware that these activities can appear to be more in line with a for-profit retail business, and you may want to avoid them. In a perfect world, you wouldn't need to advertise for memberships. Since it's not a perfect world, please observe all laws and regulations for the area in which you intend to advertise, and always consult with your attorney before embarking on a marketing program.

Referring Doctors (MMJ Only)

This should be a very powerful source for generating members. Make sure you visit all the local doctors who are supplying patients with marijuana recommendations and make them aware of your collective. Doctors will typically provide patients with a list of local collectives, and you want to make sure yours is on that list! Doctors have regulations against referring people (with bias) to specific collectives or having a financial interest (via kickbacks). You just want to ensure equal treatment and make sure your organization is known. Keep in mind that you will also be contacting these offices to verify new patients, so a good relationship is a must. Also, you may need to refer people without recommendations to doctor's offices.

Website

Building a webpage is always a good first step in getting involved in online marketing. Such a website doesn't have to be anything fancy at first (in fact, it's better if it's simple) and can be nothing more than a landing page that displays your business location, hours, certifications, and products. Maybe include a coupon code for first-time buyers to drive traffic to your actual location. Websites are pretty cheap and easy to set up. Depending on the name of your website, you can purchase the URL address and hosting for under $10/mo. Many registration websites also offer site construction tools and templates that make it easy to build your website from scratch. If you keep it simple for now, getting a website up and running can take only a few hours (or less). Make sure your site is 'responsive,' meaning that it automatically converts to mobile devices. More and more people access the web with mobile devices now, and you need to be sure your site is mobile friendly, easy to follow, and looks professional. Choosing the correct theme easily does this. Establishing even a simple website or single landing page will help people in your area find your location, which can then help drive word-of-mouth advertising and give your business an air of professionalism.

You could also write an e-book about your niche and sell it (or give it away) online. Again, this helps to establish you (or your business) as a legitimate entity and can only help make your business name more visible to the search engines so that people in your area (and everywhere else) can find your business when they type in: "marijuana sales in [insert city name here]".

Print Ads

Many collectives are choosing to advertise in local papers. All written advertising should be professional and advertise to medicinal patients only. Make sure you indicate that you are in full compliance with local ordinances and laws (be as specific if possible). For example, if you were advertising in California, you would want to reference "Full Compliance with Prop 215 and SB 420."

Before you jump straight into print advertising (which can be expensive), remember that business cards are cheap, effective, and easy to carry. As with any business endeavor, start small and grow from there.

Web Advertising

WeedMaps

WeedMaps is a website for medical marijuana dispensaries to list their current menus and specials. *WeedMaps* is a good way to get anonymous customer comments (it's kind of a dispensary-specific version of Yelp.com). Use this as a learning tool, but don't become obsessed with bad reviews, as it isn't uncommon for other dispensaries to try to discredit the competition. For that reason, it is worth trying to have negative comments removed if you feel they are unfair or unwarranted. Stay in contact with the site's administrator and try to stay in good standing with them. They will ultimately decide what comments to allow or remove.

Where's Weed

Where's Weed is a free website where you can list your medical marijuana collective. They allow you to post pictures of your collective and offer advanced features and enhanced listings for a fee.

Social Media

There are many websites available today to promote your business. Some of the most popular are Facebook, Twitter, Instagram, Leafly, and MassRoots. It's kind of weird to have to write about Facebook in an MMJ guide, but this type of social media is still on the cutting edge of marketing. This is particularly true for an entity like a collective. What better way to find like-minded people in your area? The price is right (it's free), and you can expand or contract your coverage as you see fit. This can be a very powerful resource, not only for cultivating new members, but also for providing updates to existing ones. Keep in mind that not everyone uses Facebook. Those who do, however, use it often, so it is a good way to stay in constant contact with members. If the dispensary is having a slow day, what do you have to lose by sending out an immediate special invite to members? Nothing. It's free and fast and likely to get results. Someone in your organization should be put in charge of making updates to the account every couple of days, if not daily.

Please note that traditional social media sites like Facebook and Instagram have started to push back and have banned/remove accounts associated with medical marijuana. In early 2016, Dixie Elixir's Facebook page vanished. They received a message that the page violated the site's community standards. Facebook stated, "We remove any promotion or encouragement of drug use." So we still think it is worth your while to utilize these sites; however, we suggest that you diversify your online media so you aren't overly dependent on any one site/source. Also, be aware of your content; being conservative might help your account stay active.

Unfortunately, at this point there doesn't seem to be a sure-fire way to avoid the boot from these more traditional social media sites.

Other Internet Resources

There are many ways to increase your web presence, and you don't have to rely on the above websites. This has become a competitive niche on the web, so expect new products to be developed continually. Also consider more traditional sites. Yellow Pages allows you to add your webpage, detailed information, and photos while Google has a "Places" application where you can add information about your organization. This information is then available through smart phones and other media devices.

Also try Universal Business Listing (UBL) (www.ubl.org), a local search industry service dedicated to acting as a central collection and distribution point for business information online. This will quickly enhance your web presence and save you time, because it will distribute your information to multiple search engines and websites.

You can also get the word out about your business by getting involved in the conversation and leaving comments on any number of marijuana websites. Be sure to be very professional (no trolling), use good language, and don't try to push your business every other line. Maybe once or twice per comment (depending on length) mention that you own a marijuana business, and you have had X experience. This is especially useful if you are answering questions—another great way to spread the word. The more you get involved in the conversation (and provide good advice with an air of professionalism), the more the online community will see you as an expert. This all translates to increased visibility when people in your area search online for a marijuana retailer in their area.

If you have other businesses around you (as in a shopping mall), you can always leave reviews for them on business ranking websites. Be sure to include your business information and location in the ranking so search engines can see it.

Sponsorships

Help local organizations or events while gaining exposure. Donating money or services is a great way to kill two birds with one stone. By sponsoring a local charity event, you gain needed exposure while helping out your community. This is a subtle way to get your name out, and it identifies you as a compassionate organization. Remember (as mentioned in the Pricing section earlier in this chapter), the board of directors and/or members should approve any cash donations per the collective's bylaws.

Taxes

Federal and State Income Taxes for a Not-for-Profit Corporations

To reiterate, a "not-for-profit" should not be making a profit. It is expected that the corporation will show a loss for the year. If the corporation has a profit, these funds should be distributed back to the members and management should make adjustments going forward to zero out the profit. This can be done through lowering the price charged for the medicine, adding new services for the members, making improvements to the collective, increasing wages, or a combination of those. The board will need to approve these changes, and they should be documented in the collective's minutes.

Federal Taxes

- Form 1120 – U.S. Corporation Income Tax Return.

- Due each year by 15th day of the forth month of operations (typically April 15 or October 15th with an extension, for corporations with a calendar year end).
- Form 1065 – U.S. Return of Partnership Income (and S-Corporations Form 1120S).
- Due each year by 15th day of the fourth month of operations (typically March 15 or September 15th with an extension, for partnerships with a calendar year end).
- These are new filing dates starting in 2017 (for year ending 12/31/16).

State Taxes

- Check your state's Department of Taxation website for specific information.
- Same due dates as federal return.
- May be subject to franchise tax fee.

It must be noted what could happen to a collective in a worst-case scenario:

IRS Code Section 280E

The IRS requires that you report "all income from whatever source derived." This can include illegal activities (i.e., gambling, prostitution, and drug sales). IRS code § 280E discusses "Expenditures in connection with the illegal sale of drugs," which is where they classify medical marijuana. The code reads as follows: "No deduction or credit shall be allowed for any amount paid or incurred during the taxable year in carrying on any trade or business if such trade or business (or the activities which comprise such trade or business) consists of trafficking in controlled substances (within the meaning of schedule I and II of the Controlled Substances Act) which is prohibited by Federal law or the law of any State in which such trade or business is conducted." This applies to all drug trafficking organizations (DTOs), which is how the IRS classifies cannabis dispensaries. So the IRS basically disallows all the cost of doing business. Although it sounds counter-intuitive, the IRS will allow the entity to deduct the cost of the marijuana (COGS), but nothing else. So the payroll, rent, and other normal business expenses don't count.

However, in *CHAMP v. Commissioner of the Internal Revenue Service*, 128 T.C. No. 14(2007) — a ground-breaking case with national impact — the defense challenged the IRS's position that dispensaries could not take any ordinary business deductions. The win, in this case, allowed the marijuana dispensaries to deduct most of the expenses that were needed to operate their care-giving facilities. Please note that this cooperative offered many non-marijuana services to severely ill patients.

Section 280E of the Tax Code (above) was originally designed to affect large-scale illegal drug traffickers and provided the feds with a financial weapon in the war against drugs. This code is now being used to close down medical marijuana dispensaries. In 2011, the Harborside Health Center (in San Francisco) was sent a bill for $2.4 million dollars for back taxes relating to its marijuana sales; this case began in 2010 when the dispensary's 2008 and 2009 tax filings were audited. As of mid-2016, Haborside was still fighting the IRS specifically on 280E.

With 280E still being an issue, you will want to incorporate other products and services into your dispensary. This way, you will be protecting yourself from a worst-case scenario. The IRS will allow deductions for general expenses associated with the non-marijuana services. Read U.S. Tax Court case "CALIFORNIANS HELPING TO ALLEVIATE MEDICAL PROBLEMS, INC., Petitioner v. COMMISSIONER OF INTERNAL REVENUE, Respondent" for more details.

Another alternative is to create multiple business entities (where allowable/legal).

Example: Entity #1 strictly cultivating product (which would not be subject to 280E) that sells product to Entity #2 (the dispensary) that sells to customers. When setting this up, you would want to structure it so a bulk of the expenses (as reasonably possible) are incurred and paid by Entity #1/the grow side in order to maximize allowable expenses.

Sales Tax

Sales tax is usually paid through your state's department of taxation, so be sure to visit their website to register.

In some cases, when filling out the application, you can choose not to state the products being sold. For example, in California, the following is stated: "The Board will issue a seller's permit to an applicant who does not indicate the products being sold. The applicant, however, will be asked to sign a waiver acknowledging that his or her application is incomplete, which may result in the applicant not being provided with complete information regarding obligations as a holder of a seller's permit, or notified of future requirements by the Board related to the products sold. Applicants who do not wish to indicate the type of products they are selling should leave the line, 'What items do you sell?' blank and discuss the issue with a Board representative."

If that is not an option in your state, broader terms—such as natural/holistic medicine, herbal supplement, or wellness products—can be useful alternatives.

Sales tax should typically be collected on all retail sales at the dispensary. The percentage of sales will vary state to state (and city to city), so be sure to verify that you're applying the correct amount. Laws and penalties for sales tax violations can be severe. This is an issue where the government can easily pierce the corporate veil and go after shareholders or officers of a corporation. Don't think of sales taxes as ever being your money; instead, picture it as the government's money that you are holding temporarily and transferring on behalf of the purchaser/customer.

1099s

IRS Form 1099 should be issued to everyone (excluding corporations) who is paid $600 or more (by the collective) during a calendar year. This would include your landlord, member cultivators, and any other contractors or individuals who were paid for their work.

The corporation exclusion does not apply to attorneys and healthcare providers, so you must still issue a Form 1099 to your attorney and medical doctor, even if they are incorporated. You should also issue a Form 1099 to LLCs and people operating under a DBA that you paid $600 or more during a calendar year.

In addition, collectives are required to have on file a completed Form W-9 for every person paid. To avoid having to track down payees at year's end, ask every payee to complete a Form W-9 before you pay them. W-9s can be found on the IRS website www.irs.gov. 1099s are carbon copy forms that need to be requested online or picked up at a local IRS office.

1099s should be issued to recipients by January 31, 20XX and filed with the IRS within a month (by February 28, 20XX).

Form 8300 – Cash Transactions Over $10,000

The IRS requires business file Form 8300, the *Report of Cash Payments Over $10,000 Received in a Trade or Business*, if your business receives more than $10,000 in cash from one buyer as a result of a single transaction or two or more related transactions. The IRS shares this information with the Financial Crimes Enforcement Network (FinCEN), and it is designed to combat money laundering.

Form 8300 should be completed by the person (or company) receiving the cash and is due within 15 days of the transaction. The form can be filed electronically or mailed in (to a Detroit office). At the end of the year (by January 31st), you must provide the individuals with notice that they were listed on a Form 8300. Example: You run a hydroponics shop, and John, a regular client, has one large purchase and buys $12,000 worth of new equipment in cash; you would be required to file a Form 8300 (within 15 days of the transaction). At the end of the year, you would need to provide John with a statement detailing the transactions (between the two of you) that were reported to the IRS thought the year (in this example, just one transaction for $12,000). This is similar to how Form 1099's work and report info to the IRS (except Form 8300 is for receiving money rather than paying out contractors).

The IRS has increased audits of business regarding Form 8300 or the lack of filing. There are potential civil and criminal penalties for failure to file it. The Trade Preferences Extension Act of 2015 increased these penalties. Businesses should keep copies of all filing for a period of 5 years.

Chapter 6: Other Items

Hiring Employees

Who should you hire? Your friends? A marijuana *connoisseur*? Students? Unfortunately, there isn't an easy answer. Your budget is going to determine how hard you have to work to find good employees. You can't expect to get a Ph.D. to work behind the counter for minimum wage. The two most important qualities for an employee are trust/honesty and reliability. This industry deals with a lot of cash and valuable medicine. The collective needs to be able to trust all members of the operating team. Of course, you also want to have internal controls in place to safeguard the money and inventory, but you don't want to have to police the employees.

Interview all prospective employees and prepare a list of questions ahead of time that you can ask during the interview. Rate the answers and write notes about each individual. You may need to do a second round of interviews if you don't get a standout the first time.

Friends can be difficult to work with because it can be hard to separate your personal life from your professional life. There are two theories here:

1) You enjoy being around your friends and working with them will make running the collective more enjoyable.
2) Working with your friends or family will put stress and strain on your relationship.

The potential conflicts are specific to the structure of the management team and employees. Just keep in mind that unless you have a strong (leadership) personality, it is going to be difficult to manage a friend. This may ultimately threaten your friendship.

For medical marijuana states, make sure all employees have their medical marijuana recommendation and become members before they begin to work at the collective. We do not suggest that the collective pay for an employee's first recommendation because, theoretically, only patients can become employees. It doesn't look good if someone obtains his or her first recommendation as a requirement to be an employee. Also, you don't want employees testifying that they just wanted a job and you sent them to get a recommendation. However, it should be sufficient if a patient has recently obtained a recommendation. Although it shouldn't be a huge issue, you might need to make it clear that only MMJ patients will be considered.

You should keep copies of the employee's medical recommendation, membership agreement, I-9 (Employee Identification Form), and W-4 (Employee Withholding Allowance) issued by the IRS, in the employee's file. The medical recommendation and W-4 form should be updated each year. It is possible to do the payroll yourself using accounting software (like QuickBooks), but payroll is a difficult, time-consuming process and is best left to the professionals. We strongly suggest you use a payroll service; Gusto and SurePayroll are good value options, and Paychex and ADP are more traditional full service providers. These payroll service companies should handle a majority of the state and federal filing requirements. Even so, it is a good idea to have a personal understanding of these requirements.

Workers Compensation may also be required for all employees (see local regulations). This can be expensive for a collective, especially if an employee is classified as a security guard. It will be more affordable if your employees are classified as administrative or office workers. A properly set up collective shouldn't require active security guards anyway. On average, Workers Compensation insurance will cost between 3-5% of the employee's annual wages. Unfortunately, this money is often due at the beginning of the year, based on estimates. The actual fees are then adjusted at the end of the year. You can obtain this insurance through the same provider as your property insurance or through an affiliate of (or recommendation from) your payroll processor.

Insurance

Property Insurance:

Landlords typically require tenants to purchase property insurance as part of the lease agreement. This should not be very difficult and should cost an average of $500-$1,200 a year. This insurance protects the property in case of most disasters and can cover some of the real property inside the location as well.

Workers Compensation:

As we mentioned earlier, be aware that the descriptions of employees will have a great impact on the cost of coverage; it is much cheaper to categorize someone as administrative rather than security. Be aware of the differences; if someone can be classified as either administrative or a secretary, that's a better choice than a security guard. However, there are now agents who specialize in dispensaries, and they can likely provide you with the best advice regarding this issue.

Other:

Dispensaries now have the option to insure their inventory, and cultivators have the option to insure their harvests. This is a relatively new service that is worth looking into. Unfortunately, at this point, the insurance covers only fire, theft, and robbery (not raids). A number of brokers now specialize in the medical marijuana industry, and the number of companies backing these products continues to grow. Quotes are available online.

Supplies

Keeping costs down is important in every business. You want to find a balance between ordering your packaging material in bulk and not depleting your cash flow. You want to keep your price per unit as low as possible without creating money issues or taking up too much space. You should refer back to your budget on a monthly basis and see how your actual expenses matched your estimates. Try to find areas where expenses can be cut back and also try to stay on top of your finances before you run into problems. Don't be afraid to contemplate new ideas. Research the prices of various vendors periodically to ensure that you are getting the best pricing and quality your money can buy.

Here are four traditional suppliers that offer a variety of packaging options for your medicine:

a.   www.sunpacksupply.com
b.   www.caplugs.com
c.   www.totalpharmacysupply.com
d.   www.mmjpackaging.com

Cleaning

You should rotate cleaning duties among the employees unless someone has a desire to own this activity. Your goal should be keeping the collective clean and tidy; anything less is unprofessional. Create a schedule for cleaning—it's better to do a little each day than a lot every once in a while. Cleanliness is underrated in this industry. Patients feel more comfortable in a clean environment. An unclean retail environment can lead to patients questioning the cleanliness of the products they are purchasing.

Edibles

The issue of edibles is somewhat complicated. Some states don't allow them, and some dispensaries have chosen not to offer them because they raise issues with the FDA and food safety. Many patients cannot smoke their medicine due to health problems and need an alternative method of medicating. Other patients just prefer to consume medicine for the associated body high or to avoid the carcinogens associated with smoking. Some edible options should be made available, but quality control and food laws must be strictly followed.

The THC dosage or strength of the product should also be listed on each edible item. It is common for patients to over-medicate on edibles because the effects of eating marijuana take at least an hour to manifest. Because of this, patients are unsure of the proper dosage (with a new product) and can end up consuming too much. Listing THC content/dosage is becoming more common, and some states are requiring this. Bud tenders should provide advice to patients that are new to consuming edible products.

Some dispensaries make their own edible products while others have the members or vendor make the edibles. As with all other items, please be sure you have a trustworthy source. All the products that are used for resale should be produced in a commercial kitchen and follow health and safety codes. All FDA and local food laws should be followed and items properly packaged. Ensure that all edibles are clearly marked with the following information:

"For Medical Use Only. Keep away from children and animals. Not intended for anyone under 18. Compliant with (insert local regulations here)."

Americans for Safe Access gives the following advice regarding edibles: "Problematic interactions with law enforcement may not be avoidable but (there are) things to do to lessen that likelihood. First and foremost, ensure that all edibles are well wrapped and clearly labeled 'for medical use.' If you produce edibles yourself, ensure that: a) the ingredients and finished product are out of reach of children and people who are neither patients nor caregivers; b) the facility and tools used to produce the edibles are clean and sanitary (consider compliance with local and/or state clean room requirements); and c) the packaging of edibles does not violate copyright laws nor unduly attract the attention of youth."

Chapter 7: Becoming a Medical Marijuana Patient

In states where medical marijuana is classified for medical usage, you have to get a recommendation from a licensed medical practitioner before you can purchase cannabis from a dispensary or grow it yourself. Only then are you immune from prosecution under state specific guidelines.

The medical conditions that allow for medical marijuana usage vary greatly from state to state. Some states (California, for example) are extremely liberal when it comes to getting a marijuana prescription. There you will find doctors that specifically (even solely) prescribe marijuana, and it's easy to receive a medical marijuana recommendation. Contrast that with New York where the list of medical conditions allowing medical marijuana usage is limited, and the process for getting a license is onerous; as of June 2016, there were barely 4,000 patients certified state wide per New York States' Medical Marijuana Program website.

As a patient, we urge you never to possess an amount greater than allowed by your doctor's recommendation. If you are caught with more marijuana than allowed, it becomes more difficult to defend in a court of law.

Your Doctor's Medical Marijuana Recommendation

Medical marijuana recommendations are similar to a traditional RX prescription from a doctor. However, due to current restrictions, medical marijuana is not available from a CVS or Walgreens pharmacy. The process for obtaining a recommendation is similar to an RX as well; however, not all doctors are open to this more alternative treatment. If you think medical marijuana will help your condition, then do research to ensure the doctor you are meeting is open to the idea. Another interesting difference is: a medical marijuana recommendation typically only references the amount product you can carry, possess, or grow at one time, not the amount to consume or smoke. Medical marijuana's effect on a person can vary significantly depending on the strain and ingestion method, making it hard for the doctor to recommend dosage regardless. So dosage is often left up to the patient to experiment (hopefully treading lightly with consultation from the dispensary).

Overview of the process:

- A person with a medical problem suitable for treatment with medical marijuana meets with a doctor or registered practitioner for a consultation.
- If the doctor diagnoses a condition that could be relieved by medical marijuana, they may recommend usage at their professional discretion.
- The resulting recommendation releases the patient from limitations of state law where the use of marijuana generally is banned.
- With a valid doctor's recommendation, the individual/patient seeks out a marijuana dispensary or qualified marijuana delivery service for their cannabis products.

In court, you may get away with an expired recommendation, but we do not recommend you risk it.

Doctor's Exam/Interview

Prepare for the conversation that you are going to have with the doctor ahead of time. What ailments do you have that are improved by the use of medical marijuana? What is allowable by state law? Research your condition before you go to your appointment. It may be helpful to speak with another patient who has experience with this doctor.

You should plan ahead and have a list of questions that you would like answered. The typical appointment won't last very long, so it is good to be prepared and take advantage of your time with the doctor. You may as well get his insight as well as a recommendation to use cannabis. Educate yourself about your medical condition and research what benefits cannabis can provide. In addition, certain strains of medical marijuana are likely to be more helpful in treating certain conditions. Start building a foundation of knowledge so that you can seek the most suitable treatments and better your life.

Some states may require state-issued medical marijuana ID cards, so make sure to review your state's requirements and ask your doctor about this detail.

As marijuana is becoming more accepted nationwide, the number of doctors willing to "recommend" marijuana has also grown (in some states). As the number of doctors willing to write prescriptions increases, the price for these medical examinations and MMJ recommendations will decrease.

The doctor may ask questions about your medical history and give you a form to complete if he or she has not met you before. If you are taking other medication, bring the information leaflets with you along with notes about any past illnesses you view as significant.

The interview begins with the doctor checking your vital signs (heartbeat, blood pressure, etc.). As they examine you, they will ask questions like: What is your pain level on a scale of 1 to 10?

Many doctors are already sensitive to the advantages of using natural and homeopathic cures instead of artificially derived chemicals. If you have used medical marijuana before, share your experiences with your medical practitioner. This will guide them to the right recommendation. Remember, what you tell a doctor is private based on physician-patient privilege.

The Medical Marijuana Recommendation

Public opinion concerning medical marijuana is improving daily, and there is no need to be nervous. Remember, the medical practitioner is here to help you heal. You would not be together in the same room if they were anti-marijuana.

Be aware that not all doctors work the same way. Some keep detailed records of the patients they have seen and why they felt marijuana was appropriate at the time. Others rely on copies of past medical records (or a diagnosis from a specialist or primary physician). Either way is fine and can result in a recommendation.

During the exam, the physician will briefly describe the MMJ-related legal environment in your state and advise you how best to comply with it. We recommend you listen attentively and ask them about items that are unclear.

When they're finished with the interview, they will likely have an employee draft your marijuana recommendation paperwork. The recommendation is typically good for a limited period of time (typically one year maximum). You should question your doctor if the recommendation is for a shorter period than you anticipated. You should also plan on establishing a relationship for ongoing renewals.

Chapter 8: The Heart of the Collective Model (Medical Marijuana Only)

Expense Reimbursement in Collectives and Cooperatives

Since collectives and cooperatives are supposed to be not-for-profits, reimbursements of members' legitimate expenses need careful managing. We cannot overemphasize the importance of this point. Taking out surplus cash implies you are making a profit, and that is sufficient reason for to get shut down.

What to Do with Excess Cash/Profit

If your cooperative enterprise accumulates a cash surplus, this can only be because you are charging more than the medical marijuana takes to produce and cover overhead costs. Given the competitive nature of this business, this may not be an issue. The sensible ways to deal with this are either investing in capital equipment or lowering prices until the balance restores naturally.

How to Keep a Record of Disbursements

It is highly recommended that you document all expenses/exchanges of money within the organization, especially the purchases/expense reimbursement paid for medical marijuana products (from members). Typical dispensaries obtain products from multiple cultivators. There may be specific laws or guidelines restricting or limiting who you can buy from, or who is a qualified producer. Some states expect to see an accurate record of the flowers—from its origins (the grower) to its final destination (the consumer). You cannot afford the slightest infringement of these rules.

MMJ will fall under the remit of the Food and Drug Administration as surely as will recreational cannabis. It's not a matter of if; it's a matter of when. Once it happens, the rules for sourcing, processing, and selling will be tighter. Keep this in mind as you plan for the future. See the states that already require traceability at www.biotrackthc.com/states.

Over and above these legal requirements, it makes sense to keep proper books, as any business should, so you can track cash flow and efficiency. The time will come when the government will approve the use of medical and recreational marijuana. When it does, your collective, cooperative, or for-profit entity could become highly marketable...provided that you have the numbers and prove it.

Determining Reimbursement for Member Cultivators (MMJ Only)

Since the not-for-profit dispensary model is based on expense reimbursements, this will be the core of your payments. Cultivators should only be reimbursed for the expenses they incurred while growing the medicine plus a "reasonable compensation" (which we cover in detail in the next chapter) for their time. A model dispensary will collect and file copies of all the cultivators' bills with payout documentation. Unfortunately, this procedure can be very time consuming and require a significant storage area. To make this more practical, the cultivator can complete a one-page detailed expense summary that lists all the expenditures associated with a particular harvest. [See **Attachment 3** for an example.] The cultivator will sign off on the reimbursement document acknowledging that the amounts listed are true and correct. This document also acknowledges that the cultivator will keep detailed records and receipts that the dispensary can request as needed (with proper notice, of course).

The cultivator should keep a detailed log of the hours they are allocating to each grow. Microsoft Excel, Open Office, or similar software programs can help create an organized report and reduce the likelihood of mathematical errors. The cultivator should include all direct expenses (clones, nutrients, soil, etc.) as well as allocations for electricity, rent, labor, and travel costs. Please keep in mind that compensation should be reasonable. That said, the definition of reasonable has not yet been set. In California, for example, a judge ruled as reasonable that a cultivator receive $35 per hour (the same rate as his previous job).

The labor rate is the most flexible component of the reimbursement equation. Depending on the quality of the product, the cultivator should be willing to reduce their wage to make the transaction reasonable to the collective. Travel expenses and rent allocation (if the cultivation site is a residence) are also flexible and can be adjusted within reason to get to an amount agreeable to both the dispensary and the cultivator. Nothing in the law states that the dispensary is required to accept every cultivator's medicine or is required to reimburse the cultivator for specific expenses.

Compensation (MMJ Only)

This section provides details on the salaries and/or wages of individuals working at the dispensary. In some states (that embrace the not-for-profit model), individual earnings/wages are capped at a "reasonable compensation." What is a reasonable compensation? There is no straight or easy answer. However, as with all items related to medical marijuana, you should be ready to defend your answer in court. The IRS defines reasonable compensation as "the value that would ordinarily be paid for like services by like enterprises under like circumstances." There are no real standards to go by other than similar non-profit businesses. It really comes down to the type of work you are doing for the collective, the hours worked, and the number of members you are serving. Your education level and previous employment history should also be considered. One of the best determining factors is the pay rate of others in similar occupations in similar industries. It would be hard to defend a receptionist making $100 an hour, even though that wage for a seasoned dispensary director might be acceptable. It is not uncommon for directors/CEOs of hospitals to make $250,000 to over $1M per year. In our opinion, it is unreasonable for a new collective director or founder to make a $200K salary, although it is probably not out of the question for a mature, high-volume dispensary.

Guidestar.com, an information service company that specializes in reporting on U.S. nonprofit companies, recommends the following guidance on salaries:

i) The salary/rate transactions are approved by an authorized body of the organization.

ii) The authorized body uses "appropriate data" to determine comparability prior to making a decision.

iii) The authorized body documents the basis for its determination while making its decision.

As wages increase, more documentation should be kept, including any comparative salary analysis. The board of directors will make all decisions about compensation, as discussed earlier in the Incorporating and Compliance section. The collective members should be voting on a majority of the board of directors, and they should ultimately feel comfortable with the wages being paid. The members should also have access to compensation information (in the BOD minutes) if requested. When marijuana is legalized, these guidelines will disappear, and the compensation ceiling will be lifted.

Consignment of Marijuana (If Applicable)

Depending on the finances/cash flow of the collective, it might make sense to have the cultivators provide their product on consignment, meaning they provide the product and only get paid as the customers purchase it from the dispensary. The good part about these transactions is that the dispensary doesn't need to put out any money up front for the product. The downside is that some larger or more experienced cultivators don't want to participate in this. This will make record-keeping more difficult as well. It's not uncommon to pay a higher price for consigned product (as opposed to cash purchase). Cultivators can become disgruntled if they aren't paid in a timely way, if expectations aren't met, and if product is returned. All these items should be considered and discussed before the medicine is taken from the cultivator on consignment. Please keep these items in mind, as you want the whole organization to run smoothly.

Ideally, a cultivator would be a member for a minimum number of days (i.e., ninety) before they provide medicine to the dispensary. The law may require this, depending on your location. The 90-day rule would make it possible/feasible that the product was grown after the patient became a member of the collective. Oftentimes, a new patient has excess marijuana they wish to share with the collective. (Please refer to the professional MMJ Language Section, in Chapter 9.) The courts may argue that it would be impossible for a "collective cultivation" to take place if the marijuana is already grown. If the dispensary doesn't need to participate in this activity to survive, it is better to get medicine from a small circle of patient members. The dispensary should have rules in place to ensure that it isn't violating the cultivation guidelines. Make sure to stay on top of new developments in court. You need to have cultivators sign a document vouching for the cultivation expenses claimed and stating that they personally grew the product.

In summary, select patients (those with valid doctor recommendations) are allowed to collectively cultivate marijuana for their medical needs. The more hands-on and involved every member is within the organization, the better. Unfortunately, even then you are never immune to prosecution. Make your organization as transparent as possible.

Chapter 9: Requirements of Collective/Co-op Membership

Membership Agreements

In general, the membership agreement is a contract between the medical marijuana patient and the collective or co-op. This membership agreement is the patient's commitment (and promise) that they will abide by all the requirements laid out in the bylaws of the collective. The collective must either give each new member a copy of the bylaws or have a copy onsite for review.

Most state's guidelines say something similar to "the cycle should be a closed circuit of marijuana cultivation and consumption with no purchases or sales to or from non-members." Be sure to check your state guidelines for specific language.

A California district attorney stated that "just signing a document doesn't mean anything," and that this practice is a farce. We beg to differ. As far as we know, all that an individual is required to do in purchasing a home or taking out a loan is to sign a document. Why would purchasing medical marijuana require anything different?

In a perfect world, all members of a collective would contribute the same amount of money, time, and labor, and the entire product produced would be equally split among all. However, not everyone has time, know-how, or physical ability to dig holes and/or spray neem oil on plants. The average collective member doesn't know much about growing marijuana, and you wouldn't want to touch medicine they grew with a ten-foot pole. Although marijuana does survive in many conditions, it is not easy to produce quality, healthy cannabis.

Some people want to contribute labor (in the form of growing medicine or working in the dispensary), while most members only want to contribute money to reimburse the collective. That said, we recommend that each capable member contribute some type of physical activity to the collective.

Please see **Attachment 4** for an example of a membership agreement.

Member Interaction and Community Involvement

Management needs to stay in close contact with the members. Keep a suggestion box available and encourage members to leave feedback. This allows members to leave anonymous notes or suggestions for management and is often the best way to determine what is and is not working well at the collective.

Now, more than ever, collective members need to band together. Gone are the days when all you needed was to ensure that every member had a valid doctor's recommendation. It has become more complicated to provide medical marijuana to patients as more guidelines are established. Patients should also be encouraged to volunteer for other local non-profit organizations in the name of the collective. The collective can also provide support by organizing members to volunteer for events such as a beach clean-up (where applicable), Earth Day, or United Way's Day of Caring. This is a great way to help break down the stereotypes of medical marijuana patients and solidify the collective as a positive entity in the community. If you put in hard work, it won't go unrecognized.

Documentation

The collective will need to keep current compliance and membership records available for officials to review. Given the nature of this business, it is better to keep a majority of the financial records offsite. Having hard-copy records onsite is a catch 22. It's damned if you do, damned if you don't. Hopefully you will never be raided by law enforcement; if you are, it's better that they seize as few financial documents as possible. It is better to be able to provide the district attorney with your records on your terms (upon the advice of your attorney, of course). This will help you avoid the records being misinterpreted, taken out of context, and possibly manipulated. Accounting records can be kept online; QuickBooks, as well as other secure online accounting software, is one option. There is also specific MMJ software for tracking the sales of your product. See the Accounting Section in Chapter 8 for more details.

Medical Records/Database

Patients' doctors' recommendations are required to be kept onsite securely. You can keep physical copies or save a digital PDF copy in your computer system. Databases that keep these items together for easy viewing are available, and they can be an efficient system for the collective.

HIPAA Laws

Title II of the law protects a patient's privacy by preventing the disclosure of medical conditions by health care providers, medical billing services, or insurers. Review the government's website for more information.

Other Miscellaneous Items

- You should have password protection on all your programs to decrease the likelihood of unwanted viewers.
- All city business licenses and sales permits should be easily visible at the entrance to the dispensary.
- All dispensary employee documentation should be kept onsite.

Initial Visit/Consultation with Potential Members

Membership Agreement and Bylaw Review

All patients must have a valid doctor's recommendation to become a member of the collective or enter the dispensing area of the collective. Whoever consults with potential members needs to be very thorough and detail oriented. In the old days, collectives could rush new patients in, give them the membership documents, and not be concerned whether or not the documents were reviewed. Now, procedures need to be in place to ensure that new patients understand the agreement they are signing. <u>Upon his or her signature, the signer is becoming an active member of the collective organization,</u> which may mean more than just buying medicine (as we have discussed before). In addition to signing the membership agreement, new patients should acknowledge that they have read it (with initials on each page) and sign off on the bylaws. New members should be encouraged to attend collective meetings and vote on specific issues. Members should also understand the hierarchy of the collective and who the current board members are. The new members should be encouraged to ask questions, and you should let them know that all aspects of the business will be transparent.

In general, you must be a resident in the state that you want to become a member patient and purchase medical marijuana. However, a handful of states offer reciprocity and accept out-of-state recommendations/authorizations. Note, when you are in another state that recognizes your doctor's recommendation, you must abide by the regulations for that particular state including possession limits.

In addition to not accepting out of state doctor recommendations, some more restrictive states/cities only allow local residents to be members of their dispensaries. Also, depending on the city and state in which you are operating, patients might not be allowed to purchase product on the first visit (i.e., a 24 hour waiting period). So as you can see, laws vary significantly based on location. You need to ensure that your procedures are efficiently meeting local requirements.

Verifying Doctors' Recommendations

There will most likely be a few local doctors who will be providing a majority of your members with their recommendations. You will need to ensure that each patient's recommendation is valid and check each patient's ID to verify the name and age. People have been known to create fake recommendations, and you need a process to catch these.

Depending on each doctor's preference, you can verify the recommendations by telephone or via the Internet. **Tracking the expiration dates of recommendations is extremely important.** Doing so is made easier with spreadsheets and other software programs that provide you with a warning a few weeks out so you can remind patients before their recommendations expire and give them time to schedule an appointment with their physician.

Remember, no one should be allowed in the dispensing area without a current recommendation. Don't make exceptions to this rule, as nothing good can come of it. If members protest, you have to make it clear that it is the organization's policy and that members could potentially damage the entire collective by attempting to procure product with an expired recommendation.

In addition to the recommendation, it's always good practice to make a copy of a state-issued driver's license or ID card when the member signs up.

Also, treat every new member as if he or she were an undercover police officer. This mentality will force you to go through all the collective's procedures and ensure that you aren't leaving any loose ends that could trip you up later. You don't want a reputation of having loose membership requirements; this is the equivalent of a bar serving drinks to those under age.

Medical Language

To function smoothly in the medical marijuana industry, you should get used to using medical marijuana-friendly language. Here are some examples of commonly used terms:

- "Cannabis" instead of "marijuana."
- "Member cultivators" instead of "grower" or "vendor."
- "Patient" or "member" instead of "client" or "customer."

Although using these terms might seem insignificant, it is a good habit to get into. The use of incorrect terminology (which could signify illegal transactions) can raise the interest of law enforcement. So don't create any additional burdens for your organization; it should not only be run professionally, it should also sound professional.

Chapter 10: Collectively Cultivating Medical Marijuana

Once you have your medical recommendation, you are ready to start cultivating for yourself (if allowable in your state). Your doctor's recommendation may reference how many plants you can grow. If not, check your state's law/website. If you desire to cultivate more plants than your personal allowance, then you will need to associate with other patients or join a local collective and let them know that you want to cultivate. Make sure that you have proper documentation, including a collective cultivation agreement and patient recommendations for the number of plants you are cultivating. It's always better to be over-documented and cultivate less than your maximum allowance. Keep a copy of your documentation in plain view at the cultivation site with a duplicate copy offsite. Please refer back to the **Expense Reimbursement** section in **Chapter 8** for information regarding compensation.

Plant Counts

How Many Plants Can/Should You Grow?

Allowable plant counts will vary by state, city and situation. Typically, an individual can grow a limited number of plans for personal usage. Some states allow for caregivers or a collective model, which lets individuals grow for multiple people. Calculate your allowable plant counts and have the required recommendations and cultivation agreements at the cultivation site. Always consider the pros and cons of a large plant count at a given location; in most cases, it is better to have a number of smaller cultivations instead of one large one. Smaller cultivations are easier to manage. This will also reduce your risk of robbery, seizure, and pest infestation ruining your entire crop.

Ramifications of a High Plant Count

Before 2008 (under the Bush Administration), federal law had mandatory minimum sentences for growing over a certain number of plants and other quantity-related thresholds. At that time, it was safer to keep the count below 100 plants, because going above left you open to a potential five-year prison term. Luckily for medical marijuana growers, these minimums are no longer mandatory. In 2009, Charles Lynch was convicted of federal marijuana-related charges and subject to a five-year minimum sentence. Fortunately, the judge took the specifics of the case into account and reduced his sentence to one year, specifically for selling to minors under the age of 21. As of mid-2016, Mr. Lynch's case is still in appeals.

Documentation Required

Keep a draft of the corporate bylaws and cultivation agreements at all grow operations. Keep enough recommendations onsite to cover the total plant count. Inform the members (whose recommendations should be onsite) in case the authorities question them.

Patient Cultivator Agreements

This is an agreement between the collective and the member grower. It should provide the following details:

- The number of plants being cultivated (number of patients allocated to the grow with their recommendations included).
- The policy regarding retention of records.
- The expense reimbursement calculation.
- Any product restrictions (e.g., required organic grow methods).
- Other health concerns.

- The collective has the right to inspect the cultivation site.
- The grower will abide by all applicable state laws.
- Disclaimer for liability.
- Any other items the board feels are appropriate.

Quality Control

Cultivators can have their crops tested at qualified laboratories (such as Steep Hill Labs or SC Labs) for potency (cannabinoids and terpenes), bacteria/mold activity, or pesticides. These high-quality testing facilities can also identify the presence of trace amounts of chemical pesticides in dried flowers and other cannabis concentrates.

Cultivators can also have their operations certified as organic, or as "close to organic as you can get in the cannabis industry." It is technically impossible for cannabis to get certified as "organic," because "organic" is a federally owned term, and as long as it is not a legal crop federally, it cannot be organic. CleanGreen is a program run by USDA organic certifiers. They inspect cultivations and certify farms that use organic and sustainable methods. This process starts with questions about the source of the water used, the source of electricity, how a farmer is protecting against soil erosion, the border areas (are they natural vegetation allowing for beneficial insects, or are the plants next to a toxic area, etc.), how the cultivator combats pests, weeds and diseases, and so on. Check our resources page for more info or search online to find a certification agency in your area.

Once the application is complete, an onsite crop inspection is scheduled. During the inspection, it is confirmed that the methods the grower stated in the application are in fact the methods being used onsite. There is a thorough review of all of the inputs the cultivator is using: fertilizers, pest control sprays, potting soils, etc. The CleanGreen Certified Program allows the same inputs, and uses the same input review standards, as the USDA Organic Program.

Silence is Golden

If cultivating medical marijuana is something you are passionate about, you will be tempted to tell people. Don't be ashamed; it's simply human nature. However, nothing good can come from bragging about your grow, so tell as few people as possible. This will reduce the chances that your medicine will be stolen or wrongfully raided.

Be conscious of the odor being emitted from your cultivation area. If you are growing indoors, then you want to use air filters and fans to divert the distinct smell of the marijuana. Also be diligent about what you throw away in the garbage. It is better to dispose of grow-related materials (nutrient containers, leaf trimmings, stems, etc.) at an alternative site to reduce the chances of neighbors (or random passers-by) discovering your grow.

Starting an Indoor Cultivation

Planning

Create plans for your space. It saves time to plan ahead and create the room(s) that will be most efficient for you. Talk with a mentor or a local hydroponics store to determine the best placement of your lights, air conditioner, fans, etc. You can discover some helpful information online if you are willing to spend some time researching (grow articles and associated forums). A detailed marijuana grow book will also be helpful. Don't be fooled, though; growing quality medicine is not easy. If you are new to it, be prepared to encounter pests and produce sub-quality product for at least your first few cycles. As with any skill, practice, research, and experimentation will be required. Utility and water prices will vary depending on the location of your cultivation site. Keep detailed records of your cultivation so you can notice patterns and determine how various elements are affecting your plants.

It is better to build your grow room right the first time rather than trying to get up and running as quickly as possible. You will likely need to make structural changes to the location, including adding or removing walls, cutting holes for an air conditioner, intake or exhaust, and adding electricity, drains, and plumbing. Use a licensed contractor for all electrical and HVAC modifications.

Determine the number of lights and wattage per bulb you intend to use. You will need to consult with an electrician to determine the amount of energy you have available. If you are planning on needing more than a couple of 1000-watt lights, you may need to consider having a separate electrical panel installed and running 220 volts (such as those used for large appliances like washing machines) instead of the standard 110 volts that standard appliances use. Using 220 volts will provide you with the capacity to do more work but won't necessarily save you a significant amount of money. A 220-volt system also uses bigger wires that can handle more amperage. Utility companies charge you for wattage (kilowatt-hour), not amperage. A kilowatt-hour is 1000 watts of usage for one hour, approximately equal to a 1000-watt light running for one hour. Another item to consider is the length of the wires and extension cords needed from the breaker box to the ballast; the farther away, the more resistance, which causes a voltage drop (and energy loss), which could be avoided by using 220 volts.

The basic electrical formula is: **Wattage / Voltage = Amperage**

An important consideration is safety: Is your electricity up to code? Avoid fire hazards and keep fire extinguishers onsite. Be prepared.

Expenses

Keep detailed records of the expenses associated with your cultivation. Your direct expenses would include items directly needed to cultivate (i.e., clones, soil, nutrients, electricity, etc.). You should also record the miles driven (that relate to the grow), allocation of rent (if using a residential property), and possibly some allocation of Internet and cell phone charges (if applicable). Create a log or record book to record the hours you worked on the grow, and update this log as often as possible. This will be a very valuable tool for calculating your reasonable compensation per hour (please refer to Chapter 6 regarding Compensation for more details). Cultivators are only allowed reimbursement of expenses and a reasonable compensation (which is consistent with the other collective employees or management).

Keep your expenses organized and accurate. Pick up folders and a file box from an office supply store. It is much better to develop good habits from the start instead of working hard at the end. The typical turn-around time per cycle is 8-12 weeks of bloom time depending on the particular strain you are growing. Your expenses are likely to include the following:

Start-up costs

- Structural changes (wood, drywall, insulation).
- Lights, trays, ballasts, fans, filters, air conditioner, water pumps.

Ongoing expenses

- Rent, electricity, water, nutrients, pesticides.
- Soil, nutrients, clones/seeds.
- Refer to our 'Resource Section' for a website that estimates operating costs of various grow lights.

Chapter 11: Cannabis Extraction Business

Many people see opportunity in the cannabis extraction business. There are many variations of concentrated cannabis. The common names used for the various products are hash oil wax, earwax, honey oil, butter, shatter, live resin, or dabs (dabbing). Vaporizer pens are growing in popularity; given the consistency of the product, they can be used fairly discretely, and are arguably healthier (as the product contains only the desired materials and is heated to lower temperatures than with flame).

The cannabis plant is at its most potent when it is budding, and the buds contain a higher concentration of the active, sought-after chemical compounds (typically THC and CBD). The THC level of flowers typically tops out around 20%, where concentrates can get as "high" as 80%. As such, oil and concentrates sell at a premium to dried flowers. They are typically smoked, vaped, or consumed in various edible products.

Given the relatively high price of cannabis, it makes sense to maximize the value of every plant and extract every gram of potential from it. Traditionally, marijuana trim, leaves, and shake were used to make concentrates. The demand for these products has increased as well as the number of products available. It is not uncommon for an entire harvest (including nice buds) to be produced specifically for extraction.

The simplest and safest way to extract oil is using ice-water hash bags. This method requires mixing your cannabis trimmings with cold water and ice and then straining through a series of bags that contain screens of various densities. You can produce highly concentrated THC product, which is separated in the cold environment. While this method works well for personal use, the process should be mechanized if the interest is commercial.

Cannabis extraction is potentially dangerous activity if you're not properly trained and/or using sub-par equipment. Unfortunately, it is fairly common occurrence for house fires to be started from unqualified individuals attempting home extractions. Don't plan on taking short cuts or chances in this field; we want you to make money, not regrettable mistakes.

Supercritical Carbon Dioxide CO₂ Extraction

How Does It Work?

Supercritical CO_2 extraction has been commonplace in the U.S. food industry for some time, and is inter alia responsible for extracting pesticides from vegetable crops, removing caffeine from coffee, and producing carbonated soft drinks. When passed through cannabis plant material, high pressure CO_2 separates the compounds out and then evaporates, leaving cannabis concentrates behind.

Is It Safe?

The supercritical CO_2 extraction process is automated, organic, and renewable since carbon dioxide is a naturally occurring compound. Although not a harmful solvent, the process does occur under high pressure. It follows that equipment must be pressure tested regularly, and only operated by skilled personnel with professional training.

What Does It Cost?

A CO_2 'plug and play' extraction plant can cost as little as $35,000 for a non-expandable mini version suitable for collective or minor operation. Most businesses purchase in the $75,000 to $125,000+ price range. Leasing costs and collateral can be surprisingly high, due to the 'semi-legal' nature of the industry.

Butane Closed-Loop Extraction

How Does it Work?

A closed loop system comprises two stainless steel containers. One contains butane gas (a flammable hydrocarbon) while the other is the blasting chamber holding the cannabis product. As the gas passes through the product, it releases cannabis extract, which then drips through to a collection chamber and into a vacuum oven to undergo a *purging process*. This involves the chamber being depressurized, creating a vacuum that is then heated. This process removes most impurities as well as concentrating the product. The final step is cooling the concentrated material.

Closed-loop extraction is typically used (with flash frozen cannabis) to produce live resin. Live resin has been gaining popularity (as a subset of concentrates). Live resin preserves the terpene profile of a particular strain, maintaining more genetics of the plant. Live resins are said to possess more characteristics of the base flowers including aroma, flavor, and medical efficacy.

Is It Safe

The short answer is 'yes if.' Yes, if you purchase a stainless steel closed loop system from a reputable supplier with a history in the business. Also, this requires that you employ skilled staff, leak test regularly, maintain a documented quality management system, and have the plant inspected frequently by the supplier. If you don't, then you may be taking a chance at disaster.

What Does it Cost?

A small system starts around $5,000. However, expect to pay at least $25,000 for a business application (and it can run over $125,000 for high end machines). This will include pumps, a commercial-grade vacuum oven, and miscellaneous equipment.

There are opportunities to purchase used equipment for reduced prices. Keep in mind the costs above are just for the equipment. There will also likely be tenant improvements required to get your facility up to speed.

Cannabis Testing Business

As the cannabis industry evolves, more and more testing of the product will be required. Once cannabis is decriminalized at a Federal level, the U.S. Food and Drug administration (FDA) will be responsible for edibles. Until then, this responsibility typically falls to the state departments of health, where after the Food and Drug Administration will take the lead. Unfortunately for patients, only a handful of states mandate the testing of medical marijuana; this will change over time. As an example, California will soon be implementing Assembly Bill 266, requiring product testing for: product profile/potency (THC/CBD levels), pesticides, residual solvents, and microbiological impurities (molds).

Potency Testing

The two main active ingredients in cannabis are tetrahydrocannabinol (THC), which is psychoactive, responsible for mental "high" and relaxation, and therapeutic cannabidiol (CBD) non-psychoactive with multiple medical benefits (reducing nausea, inflammation, and multiple neurological disorders).

Broad-leafed *Cannabis Indica* strains have a relatively high concentration of THC for highs, while narrow-leaved *Cannabis Sativa* is higher in CBD and valued for its sedative, analgesic, and anti-inflammatory properties.

More and more, medical marijuana patients are seeking products that are high in CBD but low in THC (and have little or no psychoactive effects). Some states only allow for the use of high CBD products for medical use. A person cannot determine a flower's CDB level without chemical testing—hence the need for these services.

THC and CBD Test

Distilling these two out to determine their prominence in a particular sample is a bit like trying to group the letters in an alphabet soup bowl.

The solution is a laboratory process called chromatography. This separates the individual components of the product by passing it through liquid or gas, in which the components move at different rates.

Both measures yield a 'score,' which, when compared with a benchmark reading, provides an indication of the relative potency of the product across the two dimensions. These are not the only cannabinoids in marijuana. However, they are the only ones that legislation prescribes.

Terpene Test

On a warm day, raw cannabis gives off a distinctive smell. This comes from aroma-emitting terpene molecules in the product. There is scientific evidence that terpene molecules interact with cannabidiol to determine the medical effects of a particular strain.

Gas chromatography is the preferred method for separating the terpenes from each other and measuring their concentration. While not specified by state law authority, terpene count is of great interest to medical providers and patients and makes a great marketing tool when describing your unique proposition. Here are brief descriptions of the five most common terpenes:

Name	Smell	Indicators
b-Caryophyllene	Woody / Spicy	Anti-inflammatory, anti-malarial
Limonene	Citrus	Anti-bacterial, anti-cancer, anti-fungal
a-Penene	Pine	Anti-asthma, anti-inflammatory, aids memory
b-Myrcene	Hops	Analgesic properties, muscle relaxant
Linalool	Lavender	Anti-anxiety and sedative effects

Tests for Safety

Pesticide Test

There are currently over 200 different (FDA approved for general farm use) insecticides, fungicides, molluscicides, and nematicides that could be used during cannabis production. Cultivators must also allow the indicated period between the last application and harvest time. By testing the cannabis, you can ensure that the product is free from any unwanted substances.

The test procedure for pesticides is the same as that for THC and CBD, namely mass spectrometry following either the liquid or gas chromatography method.

Residual Solvent Test

Some producers use butane, hexane, ethanol, and isopropanol solvents to isolate out active oils in cannabis, because this is faster than the alternative dry sieve, water, and carbon dioxide methods. In the latter case, there is still the possibility of solvent contamination via cleaning materials. This makes residual solvent testing a wise precaution. The method, as in the other instances we discussed, is mass spectrometry by chromatography.

Opportunity

We see a huge opportunity in this space. The two major hurdles are the price of entry and education required to operate. New machines will run you over one hundred thousand dollars; the facility will need to be upgraded (and maintained) to industry standards and operated or oversight by a trained professional (typically someone with a degree in chemistry). You will typically need a few machines to properly test cannabis products. Some of the standard machines include:

High Pressure Liquid Chromatography (HPLC) is used to determine cannabinoid content and potency testing. HPLC is currently the most widely accepted method. HPLC is preferred because it does not use heat in the testing process, allowing cannabinoids to be tested in its natural form.

Gas chromatography-Mass Spectrometry (GC-MS) is used for potency testing and residual solvents.

Real-time polymerase chain reaction (PCR) determines quantities of contamination, including, fungus, yeast, molds and/or bacteria in a sample, while also determining strain and terpenes levels.

These machines (new) currently range from $25K-$50K each.

Chapter 12: Delivery Services (not allowed in all states)

Depending on your location and possible bans or moratoriums, a delivery service might be the only option for you to develop a collective. The laws on delivery-style collectives are less defined than those for traditional storefronts. In fact, more and more delivery services are popping up in towns where storefronts aren't allowed. Below is a list of the pros and cons of a delivery-style collective compared to a traditional storefront model.

Pros:

- Low start-up fees
- Lower overhead
- Fewer regulations, less bureaucracy
- Less attention from law enforcement
- Flexible schedule
- More nimble operations
- Can be discreet
- Some patients are immobile (physically unable to visit a storefront)

Cons:

- Harder to get new members
- More competition
- Typically less sales volume than with a storefront
- No defined laws or guidelines
- Subjectivity by law enforcement
- Less security and higher potential for theft

"Delivery services are a relatively new creature, one that has not been directly addressed by the courts or in legislation," said Peter Krause, a California deputy attorney general who helped write the state's landmark guidelines on medical marijuana in 2008.

The same principals for starting and operating a storefront are required for a delivery service. Every member will need a valid doctor's recommendation and will need to sign the collective membership agreement and agree to follow the established bylaws. Both of these documents should be kept and filed in either hard copy or digital form. Ideally, you will keep a backup copy of these away from the originals in case of emergency.

A simple and efficient website can save you a lot of time and help streamline the processing of new members. Although not required, it is nice to have the option of an online pre-verification. It is here that potential members can scan in a copy of their doctor's recommendation, state-issued ID, and perhaps even complete a membership agreement.

Safety

Safety should be your first concern when operating a delivery service. Depending on your location, you might require everyone to be pre-verified. Another option is not to allow members to buy medicine the day they sign up. With this procedure in place, the potential member will know you aren't likely to be carrying any money or product on you. This will allow you to obtain a photo of the member (via their ID) before any medicine is distributed, and because you have a copy of their ID, there will be less incentive to steal from you. Have the potential members bring a copy of their recommendation for you or bring a laptop and portable scanner with you to make a copy. With pre-verification, most of the paperwork can be handled ahead of time. Many patients, especially the elderly and those who are very sick, aren't very technically savvy, and it will be up to you to cater to them as best you can.

Typically, the patient will pre-order/place an order over the phone (or online). Carry only small amounts of cash and medicine on your person. Depending on the scope of your delivery area, it is best practice to drop cash and re-stock your medicine multiple times a day. If you are commuting long distances, then you should determine whether a second storage location is needed.

It's a good idea to meet prospective members in public the first time. Although you won't want to meet people in certain public situations, it is comforting to know that others are around should you encounter a problem.

Some criminals view medical marijuana providers as easy targets because providers potentially have a lot of valuables — medicine and money — with them, and also because the chance of the provider calling the police is low because of the nature of the product. Storefront dispensaries typically employ a high level of security to ward off potential criminals, but delivery services don't have this same level of defense available to them. Always be vigilant and don't put yourself in any dangerous situations. **Always remember that medicine and money are replaceable; you are not.**

Clandestine Operations (if applicable)

Given the possible lack of structured state guidelines, the past actions of the federal government against medical marijuana providers, and varying opinions of local governments and law enforcement, some people may find it necessary and in their best interest to operate a low-profile operation. This might entail creating a delivery style operation rather than a storefront (if applicable), limiting the size of the entity (number of members), not notifying the local government or law enforcement, not advertising, keeping accurate accounting records (secured off site), and basically trying to be an unnoticed collective of individuals. However, you will still have to be very careful to obey all state laws, and this will likely put added pressure on you to do so. Individuals will have to perform due diligence of their specific environment and make an overall assessment of their specific situation before partaking in any medical marijuana-related activities.

Keep in mind that local police often have their own agendas and can create significant problems for you if they choose. Thankfully the overall acceptance of marijuana (and particularly medical marijuana) is growing at a rapid pace. There will be a day when you won't have to worry at all about being in this industry. Until then, stay alert, don't take anything for granted, and keep yourself out of trouble.

Chapter 13: Federal MMJ Involvement – The Last Decade or so

A New Approach for the Obama Administration (March 2009)

In March of 2009, after President Obama took office, federal Attorney General Eric H. Holder, Jr. said the current administration was taking a new approach to federal drug laws and would end the frequent raids on distributors of medical marijuana that were commonplace during the Bush administration. Specifically, "Given the limited resources that we have, our focus will be on people and organizations that are growing, cultivating substantial amounts of marijuana and doing so in a way that's inconsistent with federal and state law." Everyone in the medical marijuana industry felt this was a giant win. Finally, providers and patients could breathe easy, for a little while at least.

Federal Prosecutors Attack Property Owners (October 2011)

In early October 2011, the federal government did an about-face. At a news conference in Sacramento, Andre Birotte, Jr., the Los Angeles-based U.S. attorney for the Central District, stated that (his) Southern California region is home to the highest concentration of dispensaries in the nation. "We have yet to find a single instance in which a marijuana store was able to prove that it was a not-for-profit organization," he said.

"That is not what the California voters intended or authorized, and it is illegal under federal law," he said. "It does not allow this brick-and-mortar, Costco-Walmart-type model that we see across California."

California's four federal prosecutors also sent a number of letters to the property owners of these dispensaries, giving them two weeks to shut down. This same tactic was used by the Bush administration to successfully close a number of dispensaries in 2007. The feds can legally seize these properties through civil forfeiture if push comes to shove. According to the letters signed by U.S. Attorney Laura Duffy in San Diego, "Real and personal property involved in such operations are subject to seizure by and forfeiture to the United States...regardless of the purported purpose of the dispensary." Luckily most of the letters turned out to be empty threats.

Federal Government Closes Down Dispensaries and Threatens to Seize Property (April 2012)

In April 2012, the DEA raided and shut down Oaksterdam University, the main medical cannabis industry trade school that was founded by Richard Lee in Oakland, California. A number of dispensaries and grow facilities were also raided in Southern California around that time. In early May of 2012, federal agents raided more dispensaries and issued a number of cease and desist letters. The dispensaries were given two weeks to shut down or face criminal prosecution and the loss of property. The federal government stopped making threats and was attacking the marijuana industry at a previously unseen level.

According to Americans for Safe Access, the Obama administration unleashed an interagency cannabis crackdown that was beyond anything seen under the previous Bush administration, with hundreds of raids, primarily on California pot dispensaries, many of them operating in full compliance with state laws. Since October 2009, the Justice Department has conducted more than 170 aggressive SWAT-style raids in 9 medical marijuana states, resulting in at least 60 federal indictments.

Colorado and Washington Legalize Marijuana (November 2012)

In 2012, Colorado and Washington passed legislation (Proposition 64 and Initiative 502 respectively) making it legal for individuals over the age of 21 to possess marijuana and registered businesses to sell it. It took a few years for the states to create and implement laws for this.

Cole Memo (August 2013)

In August of 2013, the Justice Department (via Attorney General Eric Holder) issued a statement (authored by James Cole) saying that it won't challenge state laws that legalize marijuana and will focus federal enforcement on serious trafficking cases and keeping the drug away from children. The statement was directed at Washington and Colorado, outlining that the DOJ would allow the states to create laws to regulate and implement the ballot initiatives that legalized the recreational use of marijuana for adults. Federal prosecutors were issued a new set of priorities, instructing them to take a more hands-off approach. These guidelines directed law enforcement to focus their resources on preventing distribution to minors, drugged driving, trafficking by gangs and cartels, and the cultivation of marijuana on public lands. This was seen as a huge step forward for the cannabis industry.

- Recreational sales of marijuana began in Colorado (January 2014)
- Recreational sales of marijuana began in Washington (July 2014)
- Recreational usage of marijuana passed Oregon and Alaska (November 2014)
- The Rohrabacher-Farr Amendment (December 2014-2016)

In December 2014, this amendment passed as part of the Cromnibus Appropriations Bill and became part of federal law. The amendment bans the Department of Justice (DOJ) from using Federal funds to raid and prosecute medical cannabis programs that are abiding by the laws of the state. So federal marijuana laws are only enforceable if state law does not allow the activity.

In May 2016, federal prosecutors dropped a case against the high profile Harborside Health Center dispensary. The Feds had been working to seize the Harborside building in Oakland since 2014. Harborside was part of a statewide crackdown on medical cannabis in California beginning in 2011. The dispensary's founder, Steve DeAngelo, speculated that public opinion, combined with the federal loss in court based on Rohrabacher-Farr, caused prosecutors to back down.

On November 8th 2016 voters legalized recreational marijuana in California, Massachusetts, Nevada and Maine. Also, Arkansas, Florida, and North Dakota allow medical marijuana bringing the total near 30 states nationwide. This is a tipping point for the marijuana industry. More than half of the county allows the use of medical marijuana and recreational usage is becoming commonplace as well.

Federal Conclusion

Even though the mainstream view of marijuana has changed, you still need to stay vigilant, because the federal government still says one thing and does another. Fortunately, in most recent instances, the feds are solely seizing marijuana, money, and other contraband they find onsite and not pursuing criminal charges against the operators (and/or directors) of these facilities. It appears that the feds are still trying to work through intimidation. Until the Feds are 100% on board, it is something you need to be aware of; do your best to stay out of their crosshairs.

Here is the official White House stance on marijuana (taken from www.whitehouse.gov/ondcp/marijuana):

Marijuana is a topic of significant public discourse in the United States, and while many are familiar with the discussions, it is not always easy to find the latest, research-based information on marijuana to answer the common questions about its health effects, or the differences between Federal and state laws concerning the drug. Confusing messages being presented by popular culture, media, proponents of "medical" marijuana, and political campaigns to legalize all marijuana use perpetuate the false notion that marijuana is harmless. This significantly diminishes efforts to keep our young people drug free and hampers the struggle of those recovering from substance use disorders.

The Administration steadfastly opposes legalization of marijuana and other drugs because legalization would increase the availability and use of illicit drugs, and pose significant health and safety risks to all Americans, particularly young people.

The White House went on to state that, since 1996, a number of states have passed laws allowing marijuana to be used for a variety of medical conditions. It is important to recognize that these state marijuana laws do not change the fact that using marijuana continues to be an offense under Federal law.

These state laws vary greatly in their criteria and implementation, and many states are experiencing vigorous internal debates about the safety, efficacy, and legality of their marijuana laws. Many local governments are even creating zoning and enforcement ordinances that prevent marijuana dispensaries from operating in their communities. Regulation of marijuana for purported medical use may also exist at the county and city level, in addition to state laws.

As you now understand, there are critical differences in marijuana laws based on state, county, and city. For more information, refer to The National Conference of State Legislatures (NCSL).

It is important to note that the Department of Justice (DOJ) is still committed to enforcing the Controlled Substances Act

(CSA). This could change with a reclassification of cannabis but only time will tell. The Department's guidance is available on the DOJ website and provides current details.

President Obama stated that, "[He didn't] think (marijuana) was more dangerous than alcohol." Shortly after that, the White House's Office of National Drug Control Policy agreed with Mr. Obama's statement. A number of people are skeptical with Donald Trump taking over the Whitehouse. He stated that individual States should be free to choose and we have no reason to think differently. There is a lot of momentum behind this movement and hopefully he won't get in the way.

Colorado and Washington Experiment (How is recreational cannabis affecting people?)

The WA chapter of the American Civil Liberties Union found that arrests of adults 21 and over for simple possession of marijuana were down 4500% (from 5531 in 2012 to 120 in 2013). State regulation and secure dispensaries are putting drug dealers out of business and reducing teen use while adult use has not increased. Traffic fatalities and DUI arrests are down 6% and 12% respectively. In addition to those promising numbers, taxation of legal marijuana sales has generated $4.7 million in the first year of its existence. These additional funds are being funneled back into schools, drug prevention, and other programs that need funding. To underscore the benefit to the state economy, newapproachoregon.com estimates that tax income could exceed $630 million by mid-2019.

The results from Colorado are similar to Washington's. Teen use, traffic fatalities, and arrests are down considerably while almost $20 million has been generated through state-mandated tax. Like Washington, Colorado did not see any change in adult use after marijuana was made legal. More specifically, the FBI's Uniform Crime Reporting information shows that overall crime rates are down in Denver by 10% and violent crime is down 5.2%. In addition, robbery rates at marijuana dispensaries—a concern prior to legalization—have dropped since legal sales began in January of 2014. After only two years, reports show that 58% of marijuana sales now occur in the regulated market. Regulation, it seems, is doing a better job of keeping marijuana out of the hands of dealers, cartels, and kids.

After seeing the results firsthand, Colorado legislature is now working to implement the law effectively in order to further increase the benefits of the past few years. The Governor of Colorado recently signed a bill earmarking $10 million for research into the efficacy of marijuana for medicinal purposes, allowing the state to conduct clinical trials. This research will help determine which conditions can benefit from treatment with marijuana and help physicians better understand its effects. The research will also expand the knowledge base and help determine proper dosing and potency.

Final Thoughts

Starting a business these days can be a risky endeavor. But often with risk comes reward. The road to a successful marijuana business will not be easy, but the potential is infinite—you can take yourself as far as you want to go. Don't give up on your dream just because of a little hard work. It will be worth it in the end.

Going forward, keep in mind that this new industry that is set to see exponential growth in the coming years is not restricted just to the sale and distribution of the product. Sure, those things are a big part of the business model, but ancillary (supporting) industries like construction, research and development, software development, manufacturing, lending, and leasing will benefit from the coming rush. An enterprising individual with an eye towards the industry will likely be able to identify even more opportunities as they present themselves. Don't be afraid to be creative and take a chance on something that could pay off big in the end.

You now have the foundation/information you need to get started in the marijuana industry and make a run for financial freedom. As you have seen, there are some inherent risks involved, so be sure to weigh the pros and cons of your situation before you expend your time and money. This book should give you good insight into the challenges you are going to encounter while running or growing for a dispensary. Unfortunately, the rules aren't clear-cut or simple. You will need to constantly stay in touch with current news and research case laws and proposed local ordinances. Knowledge is mandatory in this industry, and you can never have too much. You can join a medical marijuana news site like www.NORML.org, www.MMJUpdates.com, or other blog to help you stay current on industry news.

Good Luck and Godspeed!

General Policies for Success:

- Research what entity type will best suit your objectives (allowed under your state's laws). Follow through on corporate requirements (i.e., bylaws onsite, monthly board meetings, etc.).
- Hire a good attorney.
- For Medical Marijuana: Make sure all members read and understand that they are members of a collective entity. Behave as if every member is, or could be, an informant. Allow only members within the dispensary, and be sure that all doctors' recommendations have been verified and kept current. No exceptions.
- Keep clean, detailed accounting and reimbursement records, preferably backed up offsite. Be transparent.
- If you operate as a not-for-profit, keep wages reasonable. The board of directors should approve and document their reasoning.
- Create an emergency plan of action for robberies, raids, and other eventualities.
- Don't keep guns at cultivation sites, collectives, or anywhere else that could be connected to these activities.
- Follow all the requirements of a normal business (i.e., sales, payroll, and property taxes).
- In the off chance you are obtained or arrested, DON'T TALK to law enforcement. Wait for your attorney.
- Don't take shortcuts when starting your business or complying with regulations.
- Make friends in the community.
- Stay current with local, state, and federal laws, and attend city council meetings.
- Have respect for your neighbors and community in general.

Resources

Visit our website at for additional information and current marijuana business news.

www.MMJUpdates.com

Organizations to be involved with:

- Americans for Safe Access, http://safeaccessnow.org/
- National Organization for the Reform of Marijuana Laws, http://norml.org

Other Resources

HIPAA Laws

http://www.hhs.gov/ocr/privacy/

Legal information (self-help)

www.nolo.com

Marijuana Strains

http://www.medicalmarijuanastrains.com/category/cannabis-sativa/

Certify your cultivation

Clean Green Certified http://cleangreencert.com/

Use code "Budding10" for 10% off "As close to organic" certification currently available for cannabis. They also offer a host of other compliance services.

Additional Cooperative Information

- National Cooperative Business Association, http://www.ncba.coop/ncba/home
- Co-ops USA, http://www.co-opsusa.coop/
- California Center for Cooperative Development, http://www.cccd.coop/

ATTACHMENT 1

Collective Expense Allocation Worksheet

Collective Expenses Monthly (Example 1)						
Salaries	6,720					
Rent	4,000					
Utilities	550					
Supplies	500					
Misc	200					
Legal Reserve Fund	500					
Total Monthly Expense	$ 12,470	(a) - Estimate				
Expected Visits/Day	30					
Average Purchase	1.5	grams	Multiplied together			
Days Open/Month	26					
Estimated Sales	1,170	grams/Mo	(b)			
Cost of Goods Sold (COGS)/Production Cost			Divided by 450			
OG Kush	$ 2,700	Per Lb	$ 6.00	Per Gram	(c1)	
Blue Dream	$ 2,350	Per Lb	$ 5.22	Per Gram	(c2)	
Big Bud (Outdoor)	$ 1,300	Per Lb	$ 2.89	Per Gram	(c3)	
Misc (Outdoor)	$ 1,100	Per Lb	$ 2.44	Per Gram	(c4)	
(a) Estimated Expense divided by	$ 12,470					
(b) Estimated Sales	1,170					
Expenses per Gram	$ 10.66	(d) - Expense allocation per gram				
So member price/gram						
Sky Walker OG	$ 16.66	(c1) + (d)				
Blue Dream	$ 15.88	(c2) + (d)				
Big Bud (Outdoor)	$ 13.55	(c3) + (d)				
Misc (Outdoor)	$ 13.10	(c4) + (d)				
These can be rounded to the nearest $1.						

Manual Daily Inventory

Strain	Beginning Inventory	Sales	Grams	1/8ths	1/4s	1oz	Total Sales* (in grams)	Add new Inventory	Expected Ending	Actual Ending^	Variance
Afgooey	222		3	1			6.5		215.5	215.5	0
AK - 47	225		6	1			9.5		215.5	215.5	0
Banana Kush	154		2				2		152	147.5	-4.5
Blue Cheese	314		5	2	1		19	227	522	524	2
Blue Dream	315		2			1	30		285	285	0
Bubba Kush	226		2				2		224	224	0
Chemdog	414			1			3.5		410.5	410	-0.5
God's Gift	112		2				2		110	110	0
Grapefruit	343		2				2		341	341	0
Headband	212		3				3		209	207	-2
Hindu Kush	454		3				3		451	455.5	4.5
LA Confidential	321		0				0		321	321	0
Lemon Drop	310		3				3		307	307	0
NYC Diesel	110		0				0		110	110	0
OG	312		5	1			8.5	454	757.5	757	-0.5
Purple Urkle	415		2				2		413	413	0
Romulan	212		3	1			6.5		205.5	205.5	0
Snow Cap	110		2				2		108	108	0
Sour Diesel	212		1				1		211	211	0
Super Silver	316		1				1		315	315	0
Total (grams)	5309		47	7	1	1	106.5	681	5883.5	5882.5	-1

5883.5
Cross Check

* **Note:** Use Excel to calculate the total sales in grams. The following equation will calculate all your standard weights to the metric system /grams.

(Column D (grams) + (column E x 3.5) + column F x 7) + (column G x 28) = total grams sold.

Once the work/equation is done, the spreadsheet it is easy to use; all that is required is to enter the number of each quantity sold, and the program will calculate everything for you. This sheet can be filled out daily or more frequently if needed.

^Per physical count

Growing Expense - Reimbursement Calculation

Sample Collective Reimbursement
Strain: Sour Diesel
Member: 128 (Mark Y.)
Date: 01/01/20XX

Note this example assumes :
1. The patient grower cultivated 24 plants on an indoor grow over a three month period and yielded two pounds of medicine.
2. * The collective is reimbursing the patient for the grow equipment spread over 6 grow cycles (or roughly two year period). This is by no means required and is an area that the board and member will need to decide on.

Clones	288	(24 at $12)
Nutrients	250	
Soil/Medium	150	
Electricity	900	
Water (allocation)	135	
Rent (allocation)	900	
Grow Equipment* (allocation)	367	$2,200/6 cycles
Travel	119	220 miles at $0.54/mile
Sub Total	$ 3,108	

Labor	90 hours	
Rate	$ 25.00	
Total Labor	$ 2,250	

Total Expense	$ 5,358

Per Lb price of the Medicine	$ 2,679

I _____ (patient # 128) declare under penalty of perjury that the information provided on this expense reimbursement spreadsheet is true and correct. I further declare under penalty of perjury that I personally legally cultivated this medicine, I am a medical cannabis patient, a Member of SAMPLE Collective and will not divert any medicine for non-medical use or for use by a non-member. I also acknowledge that I will retain copies of the above receipts (for a period of at least 3 years) as well a detailed work log. I will provide any requested documents to the Collective within 10 days of notice.

Signed:_____ Date:_____

SAMPLE COLLECTIVE, INC.

MEMBERSHIP AGREEMENT

Sample Collective, Inc., ("Collective") is dedicated to providing our members with high quality health and wellness services pursuant to (Insert state law reference). This agreement contains member requirements and guidelines to ensure compliance with the (Insert state law reference), (and the local guidelines if applicable); to protect the safety and further the health and wellbeing of members; and to continue to create a member-run, community-based, alternative healing and wellness organization.

I, _____, hereby declare and agree as follows:

I reside within _____ County and I am a qualified patient entitled to the protection of (Insert state law reference), because my physician has recommended/approved my use of cannabis for medical purposes.

_____(INITIAL)

My physician has determined that I suffer from a serious medical condition for which medical cannabis provides relief and has provided a written recommendation that verifies this fact. As a condition of membership, I have provided a copy of such recommendation to the Collective, as well as a copy of my current (Insert state) Driver's License or other recognized form of state issued identification. I understand that the Collective will keep a copy of these documents on file and will independently verify with my physician my medical recommendation that forms the basis of my right to be considered a qualified patient under (Insert state) law.

_____(INITIAL)

In order to acquire the medicine my physician recommends, and in accordance with Health and Safety Code § (Insert state law reference), I hereby seek membership in the Collective and understand that in order to be a member of the Collective, and to maintain my membership in the Collective, I must agree to and follow all terms and conditions set forth in this agreement.

_____(INITIAL)

I understand that as a member of the Collective, I must contribute finances, labor and/or resources in exchange for membership. Such Contributions are necessary to conduct the day-to-day operations of the Collective for the mutual benefit of its members, which is, but is not limited to, the cultivation and acquisition of medical marijuana.

_____(INITIAL)

I have been informed and agree that a condition of membership in the Collective requires me to volunteer (__ hours/ Month or year) in order to contribute to the day-to-day operations of the Collective, provide alternative health and healing services to fellow members of the Collectives, and/or to contribute to the overall wellbeing of the community at large on behalf of the Collective. I have been informed and understand that if I fail to volunteer, my membership in the Collective will be immediately revoked. If I am unable to volunteer as a result of my health and/or physical condition(s), I will provide the Collective a written request for exemption from the volunteer requirement and the Collective shall provide a written response.

_____(INITIAL)

I have been informed and understand that there will be an annual meeting of all members of the Collective for purposes of voting as to the operation of the Collective and that I will be advised of the annual member meeting by written notice given not less than ten (10) nor more than ninety (90) days before the date of the meeting.

_____(INITIAL)

I have been informed and understand that the Collective will make available at all times a copy of the Articles of Incorporation, the Bylaws, and any and all amendments to the Bylaws. I also have been informed and understand that the Collective will make available to me upon written request records regarding the reimbursement necessary to compensate patient-members' out-of-pocket expenses, time spent, and any and all expenses incurred in the course of growing and otherwise making available medical cannabis on behalf of the Collective.

_____(INITIAL)

I agree to be respectful at all times while I am at the dispensary and refrain from disruptive, noisy, inappropriate, violent, or rude behavior. I agree to be respectful of the area adjoining the dispensary and not deposit liter, trash or debris. I agree to refrain from disruptive, noisy, inappropriate, violent, or rude behavior in the areas surrounding the dispensary.

_____(INITIAL)

I agree not to medicate with cannabis in the areas surrounding the dispensary or on the premises of the dispensary. (If applicable in your state)

_____(INITIAL)

I understand that the Collective management has the discretion to revoke my membership at any time for any reason, including, but not limited to, non-compliance with any and all conditions of membership set forth in this agreement.

_____(INITIAL)

I agree to assign agency rights to the Collective for the limited purpose of obtaining legally cultivated medical cannabis and for purposes of growing medication for my benefit. I understand that the Collective is required to possess, transport, and cultivate medical cannabis on my and other members' behalf, and limited authority is granted to the Collective for this purpose.

_____(INITIAL)

I agree and understand that all medicine obtained is for medical use only and may not be diverted for non-medical use or for use by a non-member of the Collective. I understand that it is a violation of this agreement and of (Insert state) law to sell or divert my medicine in any way and for any reason to any other person and a violation of this section will result in immediate revocation of my membership in the Collective.

_____(INITIAL)

I agree to provide the Collective with my current medical recommendation. I understand that any member whose medical recommendation is expired shall be excluded from membership until such time that their qualified status pursuant to (Insert state specific MMJ law), can be verified.

_____(INITIAL)

I agree that the Collective is the sole and exclusive Collective of which I am a member and, further, that the Collective is the sole and exclusive source of my medical cannabis.

_____(INITIAL)

I understand that members can possess an amount of cannabis consistent with my medical need. I understand that the Collective may require verification of my medical need by way of a specific physician recommendation or through any means deemed acceptable to the Collective.

_____(INITIAL)

I understand and agree that my medical cannabis recommendation may be disclosed pursuant to any required audits by any Government agency for purposes of verifying the Collective's compliance with the (Insert state specific MMJ law).

_____(INITIAL)

I, _____, declare under penalty of perjury that the information provided on this membership agreement is true and correct. I further declare under penalty of perjury that I am a medical cannabis patient and will not divert my medicine for non-medical use or for use by a non-member. I further declare under penalty of perjury that I am not a member of law enforcement and will not divert any medicine for the purpose of any criminal investigations.

I have read and understand the above requirements and agree to follow these guidelines. Additionally, I hereby authorize the release of my medical information concerning my diagnosis, condition or prognosis to the Collective and its authorized representatives for purposes of verifying the validity of my medical recommendation and the valid operation of the Collective pursuant to (Insert state specific MMJ law).

_____   _____

Member Name   Date

_____

Member Signature

45904153R00101

Made in the USA
San Bernardino, CA
20 February 2017